*Pat Storer*

# Pot Bellies
## and other
# Miniature Pigs

**Everything About Purchase, Care,
Nutrition, Breeding, Behavior, and Training**

With 36 Color Photographs by the Author

Illustrations by Kristen Storer

BARRON'S

**Acknowledgments**

Thanks to Fredric L. Frye, DVM for his careful reading of the manuscript and to the following for allowing me to photograph their pigs:

    Cadwalder's Potbellies, Conroe, Texas
    Susan Conway's Traveling Pig Troupe, Grass Valley, California
    County Storers Ranch, Alleytown, Texas
    Lazy B Exotics, Normangee, Texas
    Ponderosa Mini Farm, Midlothian, Texas

**About the Author**

Pat Storer and her husband have been breeding and showing animals for over 33 years and training them for over 40. Pat has been an officer and board member for various animal breed clubs and show chairman for several major animal events. She is a Licensed Chief Tester for the American Temperament Test Society and has developed a temperament and aptitude test for young puppies. She has written handbooks for raising and training dogs and various exotic animals.

*All inquiries should be addressed to:*
Barron's Educational Series, Inc.
250 Wireless Boulevard
Hauppauge, New York 11788

International Standard Book No. 0-8120-1356-5

Library of Congress Catalog Card No. 92-17775

**Library of Congress Cataloging-in-Publication Data**
Storer, Pat.
    Pot Bellies and other Miniature Pigs: everything about purchase, care, nutrition, breeding, and training / Pat Storer; illustrations by Kristen Storer.
        p.    cm.
    Includes index.
    ISBN 0-8120-1356-5
    1. Miniature swine as pets.   I. Storer, Kristen II. Title.
SF393.M55S76   1992
636.4—dc20                 92-17775
                              CIP

PRINTED IN HONG KONG

45   4900   9876

**Photos on the Covers**

Front cover: Lancelot is a very special pig. Approximately 10 percent of miniature pigs are white and the other 90 percent being divided between all black and black with white.

Inside front cover: It did not take Olivia long to learn that if she rings the bell, she will get a favorite treat.

Inside back cover: Miniature pigs are easily trained to wear a harness and walk on a leash if started at a young age.

Back cover:
Top left: This is Lucy's bedroom, at the miniature pig show.
Top right: Olivia will pick up the ring with her nose and expect a small treat for this feat.
Bottom left: Oscar likes to show off his new harness.
Bottom right: Gentleness is natural at a young age for both Tabatha and the fawn.

    There are a few diseases miniature pigs are subject to that can be transmitted to humans (see page 49). If your pig shows any sign of illness, you should definitely call the veterinarian, and if you are at all worried that your own health might be affected, consult your doctor.

    Before purchasing a miniature pig for a pet, check with your local city government to be sure they are acceptable within the city's boundries. Some localities have restrictions concerning livestock. Pigs, whether miniature or not, may fall into that category.

    Leaving a pet pig alone with a dog is like leaving a cat alone with a canary. Many pet pigs have been attacked by dogs, some of whom had been living together peacefully prior to the attack.

# Contents

Preface                                                    4

**Buying a Miniature Pig**                                 5
Is a Miniature Pig the Right Pet for You?                  5
Where to Buy a Miniature Pig                               6
How to Pick the Right Pig for You                          6
Buying More Than One Pig                                   11
What Is a Registered Pig?                                  12
Crossbred, Purebred, Pedigreed,
    Registered                                             12
Types of Breeding Practices                                13
Types of Miniature Pigs                                    14
Breeds of Miniature Pigs                                   14

**Bringing Your New Pig Home**                             17
Initial Considerations                                     17
Other Pets and Your Pig                                    17
Indoor Environment                                         17
Outdoors                                                   20
Introducing Your Pig to Its New Home                       21

**When You Must Leave Home**                               23
Have a Secure Place for Your Pig                           23
Try to Find a Pig Sitter                                   23
Boarding Your Pig                                          23
Traveling With Your Pig                                    24

**Feeding Your Pig Properly**                              26

**Grooming Your Pig**                                      33
Teeth                                                      33
Bathing                                                    33
Cleaning Ears                                              34
Foot Care                                                  35

**Disease Prevention and Control**                         36
The Veterinarian: Your Pet's Second
    Best Friend                                            38
Infectious Diseases                                        39
Noninfectious Diseases                                     42
A Sound Vaccination Program                                42
Appropriate Antibiotic Therapy                             44
Giving Medications                                         44
Parasite control                                           47

Zoonoses                                                   49

**First Aid Emergencies**                                  50
Call Your Veterinarian Immediately                         50
What to Look for                                           50
Prevention                                                 58
Handling Stress                                            58
Treatment of the Convalescent                              58

**Anatomy and Physiology**                                 59

**Understanding Miniature Pigs**                           63
Rooting                                                    63
Wallowing                                                  63
Scratching                                                 63
Playing                                                    64
Defined Toilet Areas                                       64
Cleanliness                                                64
Bodily Contact                                             65
Language                                                   65
Social Dominance                                           65
"Sideswiping"                                              66
Communicating with Your Pig                                66
Your Pig's Mind                                            66

**Training Your Pig**                                      68
The Key Words in Training                                  68
Initial Training                                           69
House breaking                                             70
Establishing House Rules                                   71
Teaching Tricks and Amazing Feats                          73

**Identifying and Showing Your Pig**                       82
Identification                                             82
Naming Your Pet Pig                                        82
Starting a Mini-Pig Club in Your Area                      83
Showing Your Pet Pig                                       83
The NAPPA Standard Pig Judging Guide                       83
Tips for Showing Your Pet Pig                              86

Index                                                      87

Addresses and Literature                                   88

# *Preface*

The popularity of pigs has had its highs and lows throughout history. Various societies revered pigs as godlike animals; others sacrificed them to the gods. At one time they were blamed for carrying leprosy and other diseases. To this day, some religions reject pigs as unclean.

Pigs belong to the order Artiodactyla, which includes many other even-toed animals such as deer, camels, giraffes, antelopes, goats, sheep, and cattle. Most of the animals in this order are ruminants, meaning animals that have complex stomachs and chew their cud. The pig, however, has a single stomach much like our own.

The word *pig* has had many meanings over the years, most of which are derogatory and insulting. If you call your friend a fox or a highway patrol officer a bear, they may not take offense. Their reactions would be very different if you substituted the word pig in either instance. Nevertheless, the pig's adorable face and body shape have stolen the hearts of many people. Pig lovers who cannot have pets collect pig paraphernalia of every sort and description, from earrings to coffee mugs.

The pig's reputation for being unclean arose from living conditions humans have forced it to endure. Clean by nature, the fastidious pig has had little chance to prove this over the ages when kept in crowded areas awaiting slaughter.

The intelligent pig has long been a circus favorite in trick acts and as a humorous companion to clowns. Pigs were kept as pets by many prominent people, including Sir Walter Scott, President Abraham Lincoln, and Senator Mark Hatfield. In the past, the large size attained by commercial swine was a major deterrent to the consideration of pigs as pets. Today, the introduction of miniature pigs has shed a different light on the notion of pigs as companion animals.

Miniature pigs now appear in many zoos worldwide as part of the zoo's human–animal interaction areas. The small pigs are tractable in nature. It was not long before people who attend these zoos decided they would like pigs of their own.

In the middle 1980s, 18 potbelly pigs were imported to Canada. These were the original Connell pigs. Most of them were solid black with a few white markings. Other groups of pigs were imported over the ensuing years from China, England, Sweden, and Germany. Many of the later imports were black and white. Some were white with blue spots on the skin underlying a white haircoat.

The adorable and appealing miniature pigs were high in demand but low in supply during the first few years after their introduction. Prices skyrocketed, with some pregnant sows bringing over $20,000 at auctions and private sales. Soon, supply met demand and the price of these wonderful little pets became within the reach of anyone who could afford a purebred dog. Serious miniature pig breeders are now mating animals specifically for reduced size, without sacrificing the general health of the offspring. Many progressive city councils see the value of the pet pig as an acceptable animal within their city limits—provided the animal is neutered. Now pet pigs reside in homes worldwide. Affectionately termed the "Yuppie Puppie" of the 1990s, this is the pet to have!

Pat Storer
September, 1992

# Buying a Miniature Pig

## Is a Miniature Pig the Right Pet for You?

First, some things you must consider when evaluating an animal as unusual as a pig for a potential pet:

1. What is the initial cost of the pig you want to purchase? How does this compare to other pets you have considered? Have you shopped around and compared animals and prices?
2. If you are buying a piglet, what is the animal's projected adult size? Can you see the pig's parents? Is this a size that will be comfortable for you and your family, given your living conditions?
3. What is the average life span for this type of pig? If it is a very short one, is it worth the initial expense? If it is a very long one, are you willing to commit that length of time to the pig's physical and mental well-being?
4. Has the pig been kept clean? Will it use a litter pan, or be easily house-trained to go outdoors?
5. Do you have outside facilities for exercise and for grazing by pigs? If you intend to keep you pig indoors most of the time, do you have time to take it for walks?
6. Is the animal intelligent? Is it easily trained?
7. Will a pig be compatible with all members of the family, and occasional visitors?
8. Can a pig be integrated with other household pets you may have?
9. What is the estimated monthly cost of food and the availability for its purchase?
10. What grooming is necessary?
11. Does the pig need to be immunized or dewormed? Are you familiar with diseases and parasites that affect pigs? Can you find a veterinarian who will treat pigs and keep your pet current on immunizations?
12. Are you aware of any unusual habits pigs might have that would not be acceptable behavior for your lifestyle?
13. Do pigs harbor any diseases or parasites that might be transmissible and harmful to humans?
14. What will you do with the pig when you leave the house?
15. Who will care for the pig if you leave for extended periods (vacations, illness, etc.)?
16. Will you neuter your pet? Do you know what that will cost?
17. Will you breed the pig? If so, do you fully understand what this entails? Are you ready to accept the responsibility of finding good homes for the offspring?
18. Are you familiar with city/county ordinances regarding pets?
19. Are you willing to take the time necessary to train the pig to be a responsible member of your family and community?
20. Have you asked other people who have pet pigs how they rate them as a pet?

Answer the above questions and decide if you really want to buy a pet pig. Read the sections of this book on the different breeds of miniature pigs, what sex to choose, and getting ready to bring your pet pig home. When you have done this homework, you will be well prepared to choose a pet pig. Should you decide to proceed, bear in mind that buying a pig for a pet can be a long-term responsibility. Due to disease and predators, pigs seldom reach the age of 15 years. But the life span of a well-cared for house pig can be up to 25 years. Buying a pig as a pet for your children can be a responsibility that you yourself must assume someday. Eventually, your children will reach adolescence and have other interests outside the home; soon afterward, they will leave for college and careers. The pig will still have many years left and you must be willing to care for it into its later life.

## Where to Buy a Miniature Pig

Where can you buy a pet pig? How can you select one that will make a good pet? Start by doing some research. Check the classified section in your local newspaper under "Miscellaneous Animals" or "Exotic Animals." Write to or call one or more of the miniature-pig registries and ask for names and addresses of breeders located near you. Check local pet stores and feed stores. Some have pet pigs or can get them for you. Perhaps they have connections with breeders that supply them.

Next, visit breeders, feed stores, and pet stores that specialize in pet pigs. Look over their stock carefully. Are the pigs living in clean surroundings? A pig from a clean environment will be easier for you to housetrain. Are their eyes clear? Are their skin and coat free of flaking skin? Does the seller offer a health guarantee? Will you have time to get a veterinarian's advice on your purchase? Are you furnished by the seller with health records for immunizations, vaccinations, and deworming? Are you given, at time of purchase, either a registration certificate or individual litter registration certificate for the pig? Are the animal's parents or pictures of the parents on the premises? Has the pig been properly socialized and handled since birth? Does it con-

tinually squeal when you pick it up? Does it try to bite?

## How to Pick the Right Pig for You

Do not buy a pig on an impulse—because it is cute and irresistible, for example. Take the time to get to know the pig breeder's stock and handling methods. If that is not possible, spend as much time as you can with the pig you want to take home.

### Temperament

Be sure that the breeder has socialized the pig properly before you purchase the animal. It is important that the breeder has handled the babies almost every day from birth. A piglet that is familiar with handling will be easier to train and less stressed when you or your veterinarian needs to hold it.

Can you pick up the pig and hold it? Many pigs will squeal for a moment or two when picked up, a natural behavior inherited from wild ancestors. The quiet, passive piglet made a lovely meal of young pork for a happy predator. When a piglet squeals, do not take it as a personal rejection. A well-socialized piglet will quiet down after a minute or two. If the piglet does not scream when the breeder picks it up but does when you hold it, don't despair. This behavior indicates that the piglet is bonded to the breeder; the animal will normally transfer this bond to you within a few days. If the piglet does not quiet down in that time and continues to squeal or scream, you might want to choose another one.

### Health and Conformation

How do you choose a pig that will be a good pet? Here is a checklist that may help:

# Buying a Miniature Pig

1. Check the general health of the pig.
   - Is the pig bright and active?
   - Are its eyes clear and free of matter?
   - Is its nose free of discharge? A small amount of clear moisture on a pig's nose is normal.
   - Is the pig in good shape—not too fat, not too thin?
   - Are the pig's hooves properly trimmed and free of fungus?
   - Is the skin supple and free of excess flaking? (A small amount of flaking is not harmful.)
   - Are the ears clean? Are they without a foul odor?
   - Are the teeth straight and clean?
   - If you can see a bowel movement, is it firm and free of visible worms?

2. Will the seller provide you with a complete record of vaccinations, immunizations, and deworming schedules?

3. Is there a health guarantee? Ask the seller if you can take the pig to your vet for a physical. If your vet finds any serious problems, will the seller give you a full refund or exchange? If your veterinarian feels that a replacement would not be a good idea due to contagious disease or hereditary faults, will the seller give a full refund?

4. Does the seller have the pig marked with permanent means of identification, such as a microchip, tattoo, or ear tag?

5. If the animal is registered, will the seller provide you, at the time of sale, either a litter registration certificate or a certificate of registration?

6. How gentle are the pigs from which you have to choose? Many piglets and older pigs in a group will band together. Isolating a pig that appeals to you will give you a better idea of its nature. Ask the seller if the pigs bite, and ask him to catch the pig. If you select a pig that squeals when the breeder catches it, do not despair. It is the length of time the pig continues squealing that is important. Piglets that have been properly socialized will not squeal at all, or will squeal for 30 seconds or less when first caught. If the pig takes a long time to stop squealing or doesn't stop at all, resign yourself to the fact that this pig will take a lot more work than the nonsquealer to make the wonderful house pet you are anticipating. If the pig tries to bite, even nip, cross it off your list immediately. Good disposition is imperative.

7. Find out if the animal is neutered. Neutered animals are the best buy for pets.

8. Check the conformation of the animal. Not only should it should meet the description for the specific breed, but it should be generally sound.
   - The legs should be sturdy, with the toes pointing forward.
   - The pig should have two toes of equal length, with two dewclaws on the rear of the foot that touch the ground only when the pig is moving at a high speed or on a soft surface.
   - The rear legs should be set widely apart, with the hocks straight or pointing inward *slightly*.
   - The chest and shoulders should be well developed.
   - The rump should be well rounded on females, a bit narrower on males.
   - There should be balanced muscling.
   - The pig should walk with good width between its legs.
   - The pig should move freely, without lameness.

9. Compare the pig to littermates or pigs

of the same breed and age. A genetically small pig with proper conformation will make a more acceptable house pet.

10. If all the above conditions have been met, then—and only then—pick for cuteness and color.

## Sex

Several factors determine whether you should purchase a male or female pig:

- Consider the reason you are buying the pig (pet only, showing, breeding, etc.).
- Is it to live in the house with you?
- Do you want to teach it tricks?
- Is it to live outside or in a barn?

Many people feel that a pet must reproduce to feel fulfilled. We cannot speak for the pig, but it probably will not be practical for you to have a pig as a household pet that is also having babies. You must decide if you want a pig to live in the house with you and only occasionally go outside to graze, or a pig that is to become a breeder. If you want a pet and also want to have baby pigs someday, you will need one pig for each purpose.

The closer you want to live with your pigs, the more you must discourage the sexual side of its life. In short, neutered pigs make the best household pets.

**Sexually Intact Pigs:** *Boars*, even as very small youngsters, begin to get the telltale boar odor that is irresistible—but only to female pigs. This odor gets stronger and longer-lasting as the boars get older. It is something you do not want anywhere in your house, especially rubbed into your plush carpet or your favorite chair. I doubt that many people at your office will offer you a luncheon invitation if your pet boar slept on your shoes last night. The boar odor is on the animal's breath and is also cre-

ated in a special little sac in the sheath that houses the penis. All sorts of pungent liquids collect in this sac, like old urine, hormonal secretions, and other debris. When the boar rubs his belly on anything, lies down, or urinates, he leaves behind his telltale mark.

Boars tend to mark ownership of places and objects with this odor-producing substance. Anything they consider belonging to them, or things they would like to belong to them, are "stamped" with this scent. This can include you, other pets, and your mother-in-law.

Boars that have been left sexually intact have an extremely high libido and will "practice" on other boars, unwilling female pigs, your leg, other household pets, and small children. When these objects are not available, the boar may choose inanimate objects such as toys, pillows, feed dishes, or anything it can manage to corral.

If you find a little boar that you cannot resist, consider having your veterinarian neuter him right away. If you must have this pig and decide not to neuter him, your choices are few. Make him a place in the barn to live, or realize that you and everything you own will be marked by him and attractive to every little sow within fifty miles. Intact males are not suitable house pets.

*Gilts and Sows* are sexually intact female pigs. A gilt is a young female pig that has never given birth. A sow is a mature pig that has had one or more litters. Most female miniature pigs begin their reproductive cycles as early as three months of age. Then, every 21 days, the hormones in the body of the female control

Properly socialized miniature pigs are rarely aggressive. Top: Children should be taught to respect the pig's amiable nature and to treat them with kindness.
Bottom: Introduce piglets at a very young age to non-aggressive animals.

her actions for 72 hours. The female pig can and usually will become moody, restless, and irritable during this time. Even if you are sure she is housebroken, she probably will "forget" during this time. Like the male, she will mark places with her scent so any boar that shows up can track her down. Although she knows that no boar lives in the house, her instincts tell her that she must leave messages around, just in case!

A sow should be kept sexually whole only if the intention is to breed her someday. But the decision to keep a breeding animal must be made carefully; raising a litter of pigs in the house is no bed of roses.

**Altered-sex Pigs:** Neutering of boars can be done as early as two or three days of age. Breeders who deal in pet pigs probably will have this done before you buy. When done at this early age, it is a somewhat simple procedure. The breeder or your veterinarian may use a general or local anesthetic.

Castration of any pig with a potbelly must be done with utmost care by a veterinarian who is familiar with this procedure. These pigs have large inguinal rings through which the testes may retract or the intestines may protrude. If the boar retracts the testes before the vet has had a chance to remove them, this will complicate the surgical procedure. If the inguinal rings are not sutured shut after castration, the intestines may protrude through the openings due to pressure caused by the large volume of organs in the abdomen.

Recovery from castration is very quick. The

Much about the pig's attitude can be determined from the position of its ears. If they are in the normal position, the pig is relaxed and comfortable. Ears drawn back toward the neck may indicate apprehension or uneasiness.

neutered pig (called a barrow) has little discomfort and goes about its business immediately after the procedure, or when he awakens from the general anesthesia, if that is used.

Spaying of gilts can be done as early as six weeks of age. This procedure should·be performed by a veterinarian familiar with the internal structure of the pig. If the gilt is a potbelly, it is best that she not be overweight. A fat gilt carries much fatty tissue in her belly, which will cause difficulty for your vet during surgery and excess pressure on her sutures afterward. Spaying procedures can be done that remove only the ovaries, or that are complete hysterectomies. Recovery from spaying takes a few days for a gilt, during which time she should be kept exceptionally clean and dry.

Neutered barrows or gilts housebreak more easily and make better house pets.

## Buying More Than One Pig

Many people feel that when they get one animal, they should get another of the same species to keep the first one company. It may sound compassionate to let your pig have a friend to play with, but you will be defeating the purpose of having a pet of your own. When given a choice, a piglet will choose another piglet to play and bond with before it will choose a human. I doubt that your wish is to have a pig who has a pet pig.

After a piglet has grown up with and bonded to a human family, you can add another pig if you wish. But if you wait too long, the original pig may begin to act aggressively toward the newcomer who is invading its territory. Neutered pigs have the least problem adjusting to additions to the family. So, for your first experience with a pet pig, pick only one.

# *Buying a Miniature Pig*

## What Is a Registered Pig?

Before you decide whether or not to buy a registered pig, you should understand certain breeding terms that may be used by the seller. The terms "crossbred," "purebred," "pedigreed," and "registered" may be confusing to people who have never owned an animal or who have owned an animal of mixed parentage. These terms refer to the history of the individual pig's parentage.

## Crossbred, Purebred, Pedigreed, Registered

**A crossbred animal** is the product of two distinct breeds of animal—for example, a Vietnamese potbelly and a guinea hog. There are no mutual relatives. They are not purebred, pedigreed, or registered. Crossbreeding can occur by mistake, or with specific intentions. New breeds are created by crossbreeding one or more breeds for specific traits to produce a new breed. This takes many generations—and much dedication and expertise on the part of the breeder.

**A purebred animal** is a member of a breed that possesses a common ancestry with distinctive characteristics. Purebred animals also may be pedigreed and registered, but not necessarily so.

**A pedigreed animal** is a purebred whose family tree is documented. It has been chosen selectively for that particular mating. It may be registered, but not necessarily so.

**A registered animal** is both purebred and pedigreed. It is eligible for registry or is already registered with an association that maintains pedigree records for that breed. This organization controls and maintains all records about pedigrees and registration certificates for each animal of the breeds for which they are recognized. A registry may be established for controlling pedigrees of more than one breed. Or there may be more than one registry organization for a breed or group of breeds. There is one main multibreed registry for miniature pigs, three registries for potbelly pigs, and several for other individual breeds.

## Why Buy a Registered Pig?

There are several points to consider when deciding whether to buy a registered pig:

1. A registered pig has a well-documented family tree.
2. A registered pig comes with:
   - A registration certificate, or
   - An application for registration. This form must be signed by the breeder and mailed by the buyer to the registry. Usually the pig's name has not been chosen, and the selection of a name becomes the privilege of the buyer. The application does not ensure issuance of a registration certificate by the registry. Normally, measurements and photographs must be furnished by the buyer to the registry. The registry will then decide if the pig is eligible for registration and issue a certificate or letter of denial.
   - You cannot produce registered piglets from nonregistered parents.
   - Registered pigs usually cost more than ones without registration papers.
   - Nonregistered pigs may have a questionable heritage. You have only the breeder's or seller's word to believe.
   - Registered pigs usually have some form of permanent identification to distinguish one pig from another.

• Only registered pigs may be shown at shows sanctioned by pig registries.
• If you have a pedigree on a registered pig, you can research the family tree to find sizes, show records, color, etc.

Contact each registry for information and evaluate their qualifications yourself.

If you plan to purchase a registered miniature pig, you should be shown papers from one of the registries listed in the back of this book. If someone tells you, "I can get the papers on this pig," believe it only when you see the papers.

After purchasing a registered pig, look over the pedigree. You can probably figure out if the breeder selected parents for specific traits, or to establish a type by using inbreeding and linebreeding (see next section).

## Types of Breeding Practices

### Inbreeding

Inbreeding includes matings between father and daughter; mother and son; or sister and brother. Because of the close or duplicate ancestors, inbreeding doubles up desirable and undesirable traits. A brother/sister mating involves only one pair of grandparents instead of two, for example. Recessive genes are hence doubled and manifested in most of the offspring.

### Linebreeding

Linebreeding includes matings between close relatives by matching pedigrees and choosing ancestors (other than those mentioned above) that carry the specific traits desired in the offspring. For example, uncle/niece; grandfather/granddaughter, cousin/cousin.

Both of the above-mentioned practices are termed "closebreeding" by some.

**Results of Inbreeding and Linebreeding:** Although many breeders avoid these methods entirely, there is a lot to be said for carefully choosing mutual ancestors.

1. The resulting offspring are more pure and uniform in structure to each other.
2. Breeders can set their "type" by developing their own strain and "look," unique to their herd.

Before inbreeding or linebreeding, a breeder should consider several things:

1. The animal's worst traits will be more evident.
2. Rigid culling will be necessary to remove undesirable traits in future generations.
3. The offspring may have reduced reproductive quality.
4. Hybrid vigor (vitality of the crossbreed) will be greatly reduced. This is a depression of the immune system that will leave offspring susceptible to a greater number of diseases.
5. Abnormal weight gain due to food-assimilation abnormalities may occur.

It is important that a breeder select miniature pigs for small size, cuteness, and color. Equal attention should be paid to the qualities that make the pigs genetically hardy, such as their strength, disease resistance, ability to reproduce themselves, and success in raising their offspring. Size or color should not be the prime consideration in raising or choosing any animal, especially diminutive types, because many genetic mistakes are manifested in stunted growth. These defects can be passed on to immediate and future offspring.

# Buying a Miniature Pig

## Types of Miniature Pigs

### Categories of Miniature Pigs

Miniature pigs fall into two categories (body styles): midget and dwarf. Although both types are smaller than normal animals of the same breed, there are distinct and important differences between them.

**A midget** is a representative of a particular breed of animal that is much smaller than normal but is *proportionally correct internally and externally*. This means that if the animal is 50 percent smaller in size than normal, the heart, liver, feet, eyeballs, etc. are all 50 percent smaller than normal as well.

**A dwarf** is a representative of a particular breed of animal that is much smaller than normal but is *not proportionally correct*. A dwarf has shorter limbs, a larger trunk, and a larger head in proportion to its body size. The most important aspect of this reduced size is that most of its internal organs will be proportionately larger than those of a midget of the same size; they will be nearer to the same dimensions of a normal-sized animal of its species. This accounts for the larger trunk in these animals and the "potbelly" in some breeds of pigs. This means that an animal that is 50 percent smaller than normal size will have the heart, liver, and other internal organs closer to normal size.

**Standards:** The American Miniature Pig Association (AMPA) has set the size limits for miniature pigs at 125 pounds (56.8 kg) maximum weight, 22 inches (55.9 cm) maximum height. Miniature pigs weigh between 8 ounces and 16 ounces (227–454 g) at birth. Two factors contribute to the adult size of the pig: genetic makeup and nutrition. (This will be covered in detail later in the book.) True miniature pigs, at adulthood, are usually between 10 inches and 16 inches ( 25.4–40.6 cm) in height. They weigh between 20 pounds and 95 pounds (9–43 kg) if they are in proper condition and are not fat. Some pigs sold as "miniatures" have eventually tipped the scales at up to 200 pounds (91 kg). The reasons for the large size can be overfeeding, improper feeding, or crossbreeding. Perhaps only one parent was a miniature, or both parents were at the top end of the scale for miniatures.

It is important to know your breeder, if possible. Ask the person selling the pigs for a registration certificate on the pig you would like to buy. Not all miniature pigs that are for sale are registered. Whenever possible, ask to see the pig's parents. If you have the opportunity to pick from a litter, use size, health, and conformation as your first criteria in making your choice. If any of those elements are not exactly what you want, look around some more. Ask about the size, weight, and age of the parents. Ask if there are any full or half siblings from previous litters for you to view. If you are buying your pig at a pet store or from a breeder with only one pig to show you, ask to see pictures and the registration certificate on the pig and its parents. There are three registries for miniature pigs, all of which set maximum size limits. Reputable breeders of registered miniature pigs are constantly trying to reduce the size of their offspring, while still maintaining healthy, genetically viable stock. You stand a better chance of having a genetically small pig from proven registered parents.

## Breeds of Miniature Pigs

Currently, there are five distinct breeds of miniature pigs

- Vietnamese, also called potbellied
- Juliani, also called painted miniature

# *Buying a Miniature Pig*

- African pygmy, also called Guinea hog
- Yucatan, also called Mexican hairless
- Ossabaw Island

## Vietnamese (Potbellied) Pigs

This breed of pig has long been a favorite in zoos around the world because of its appealing appearance and docile disposition. The general features of a potbellied pig are an exaggerated potbelly, swayed back, erect ears, and a straight tail. Today, this is the most popular miniature pig kept as pets.

The potbellied pig's maximum acceptable height, measured at the withers, is 18 inches (45.7 cm), with the ideal height less than 14 inches (35.6 cm). The length should be in proportion to the height.

The maximum allowable weight is 95 pounds (43 kg), with the ideal weight less than 50 pounds (20 kg) . Today's breeders are producing tiny toy pigs that are under 30 pounds (13.6 kg).

The nose is short to medium length. Many people prefer a pugnose appearance. Do not choose a pig with a nose too short; it may have difficulty breathing because of deformed nasal passages.

The acceptable colors are all-black, all-white, or black-and-white pinto pattern.

## Juliani (Painted Miniature) Pigs

This breed of pig was imported to the United States from Europe after years of selective breeding for small size.

These pigs have small to medium-size ears, a slight potbelly, short hair, a swayed back, and a short, straight tail. Their colors can be red, red-and-black, red-and-white, white, white-and-black, black, silver and silver-and-white. Their legs are longer than those of the potbellied pig. They range from 15 to 60 pounds (6.9–27.3 kg) and 10 inches to 16 inches (25.4–40.1 cm) in height.

Juliani pigs have a gentle disposition and love to play, especially if they have someone or something with which to play.

## African Pygmy (Guinea Hog)

History tells us that this breed of pig was brought with the slave trade from Africa to the southern United States. Originally, this was a breed of huge, red hairy pigs. What we call Guinea hogs today have evolved into a small black pig.

These pigs, which live up to 25 years, are usually 14 inches to 22 inches (35.6–55.9 cm) tall. Their weight limits are 40 pounds to 60 pounds (18–27 kg), with the preferred range between 20 and 40 pounds (9.1–18.2 kg). They are not dwarfs, but true midgets.

They are not swaybacked, nor potbellied. They are shorter in the forequarters than the hindquarters. They have a moderately short snout and a slight bristling and thickening at the nape of the neck. Most of these pigs are active, alert, and highly intelligent. They have straight backs, a kink in their tails, medium-sized ears, and smooth, nonwrinkled skin with bristly hair. They are stocky, with short legs. The breed is recognizable by its shiny black coats, which may have white markings.

African pygmies prefer grazing on lush grasses instead of rooting for their meals. They are normally docile and get along well with each other, other household animals, and humans. They bond readily to humans and prefer to be close to their favorite people.

African pygmies have their own registry, and are also registered by the American Miniature Pig Association.

# *Buying a Miniature Pig*

## Yucatan (Mexican Hairless) Pigs

This gentle breed of pig originated in Mexico and Central America. They have straight backs and bellies, short snouts, sparse haircoats, medium-sized ears, and they are slate gray to black in color. They are often used in laboratory testing, since their skin, cardiac, and other systems resemble those of humans.

There are two sizes of Yucatan pigs. In the larger type, males weigh up to 200 pounds (91 kg) and females up to 180 pounds (82 kg).

Laboratories have bred for a smaller type and have produced the miniatures that weigh between 50 pounds and 100 pounds (22.7–45.5 kg). Heights on these animals range from 16 inches to 24 inches (40.6–61 cm).

## Ossabaw Island Pigs

Ossabaw pigs are categorized as "feral." A feral pig is defined as stock that has been running wild at least one hundred years with no introduction of domestic or other outside blood. The colonists who settled Georgia brought them for food. They possibly represent the primitive pariah-type village pigs of medieval Europe. On the mainland of the United States, they crossed with many domestic breeds, but the strain is believed to have remained pure off the Georgia coast on Ossabaw Island. There the genetically small size developed by "insular dwarfism."

Ossabaw pigs have long snouts, heavy coats, and ears that stand upright. The desirable height is 14 inches to 20 inches (35.6–50.8 cm), with weights of 25 pounds to 90 pounds (11.4–41 kg). Ossabaws can reach a weight of 250 pounds (113.6 kg) in captivity if improperly fed.

These pigs exhibit a wide variety of colors. There are solid colors, including gray, blue, red, and, in rare instances, white. They also come in spotted, striped, and calico patterns of black-and-white, red-and-black, and black-white-red. Although striping does occur in the young of most pigs of wild origin, it does not occur in the babies or adults of this breed.

Ossabaws have excellent temperaments; they are very lively, friendly, and extremely intelligent, perhaps owing to their wild heritage. They are easy to train and will bond with all members of the family, including other pets. Their life expectancy is up to 25 years.

*Important note:* Ossabaw pigs have a low-grade form of diabetes and are known to be the fattest wild mammal in the world. They have a unique system of fat metabolism. During low-food-supply periods, they live off the fat stored in their bodies. They are useful as laboratory animals in the study of human nutrition, obesity, and diabetes.

### Taxonomic Classification

**Class:** Mammals

**Subclass:** Eutheria (higher mammals as opposed to egg-laying mammals or marsupials)

**Order:** Artiodactyla; (Even-toed Ungulates) includes Swine, Peccaries, Hippopotamuses, Camels, Deer, Giraffes, Cattle, Goats, Sheep

**Suborder:** Nonruminantia or Suiformes (nonruminants) includes swine and peccaries

**Superfamily:** Suoidea

**Family:** Suidae (Old World Pigs)

**Genus:** *Sus* (Wild Boars)

**Species:** *Scrofa domestica* (all domestic breeds)

**Subspecies:** Asian Domestic Pigs (includes masked pig, Vietnamese pig, Papuan pig)

# *Bringing Your New Pig Home*

## Initial Considerations

Before you bring your new pig home, consider the following:
- Realize that while housebreaking the pig you must *never* leave it unsupervised in the house.
- Decide the method of house-training you will use.
- Plan a location for the pig's nursery and get it ready.
- Decide if the pig will have access to the outside.
- Provide an outside pen, if possible, when you will be gone for long periods of time.
- Read closely the sections in this book on training and understanding your pig.
- Evaluate the compatibility of the pig with other pets in your home.

Do *not* take time off from work to be home while the pig adjusts. If you work all day, plan to get the pig on a weekend, if possible, and return to your work schedule on Monday. If the pig gets used to your giving it attention all day for two weeks, it will be upset with the change when you eventually leave it alone.

## Other Pets and Your Pig

Pigs normally have little trouble with other pets in the home; however, your current pet(s) may not have the same feelings or intentions. Cats are rarely affected by the introduction of a pet pig into the home, but dogs that are aggressive or very rambunctious are not suitable companions for pet pigs. The behavior of your other pets with respect to your pig must be monitored carefully at all times. Even a gentle dog can have its wild instincts rise to the surface when it hears the scream of a pig in distress or the pig tries to take some of the dog's food or toys. Never leave your pig and dog(s) together without close supervision.

## Indoor Environment

Pigs are creatures of habit and do not like change. Therefore, you should have everything ready for your pig before you bring it home. Then, when the pig enters its new environment, everything will be in their permanent locations.

Before you bring your pig home, determine where you will want to train your pig to relieve itself. You can teach it to use a litter pan or a doggie door. You also can train it to let you know when it wants to go out. Training methods are discussed under "Housebreaking," page 70.

If you plan to train to use a litter pan or a doggie door, be sure to have it ready for use *before* you bring your pig home. Changing training methods midstream is counterproductive and confusing to the pig. Like pigs in the wild, domestic pigs are true creatures of habit and will soon form a "path" to their potty area.

When you first bring your pig home, you

A bed for your pig can be a large basket or half an airline crate. Line the bed with washable blankets.

probably will confine it either to a playpen or one room in your home until it is well housebroken. Wherever you place the bed then should be its permanent location. If you must move the bed later, do so a small distance at a time until you have reached the new location.

• Pick this initial spot carefully.
• See that it is free of drafts.
• Be certain that no heat blows directly on the crate. Check for nearby heat exhausts from vents or appliances.
• Do not place the bed in an area where there will be a great deal of traffic. Your pig will have nap times and bed times when it will not want much action around it.

Get the bed ready. Pigs like to nest in leaves and grass outside, but you can substitute towels and blankets for these materials if your pig is to live in the house. You can use a well-constructed soft dog bed that is washable. Add a few towels or small blankets and maybe a small pillow or stuffed animal. Half of a travel transport for pets, about twice the size of your pig, also makes a good bed. It can be washed outside with a hose, or in your bathtub.

## Pig-proofing Your House

Check your house for poisonous substances and dangerous items within the reach of your pig. (Consult the poisoning and injury sections of this book for a complete list.) Some things to look for in your home are toxic houseplants, accessible electric plugs, open low garbage cans, chemicals of any nature, and cupboards with loose doors.

With their acute sense of smell, pigs find all the world a potential meal. Your pig will learn quickly to open loose doors and then decorate your house with the contents. Things not

Use dishes that are tip-proof. The dish on the left is easily spilled by a hungry or thirsty pig. The structure of the middle dish, made of crockery, and the dish on the right, made of stainless steel with rubber edge strip make them very difficult for a pig to overturn. They also can be easily cleaned.

harmful to us can be harmful to pigs. A few things to look out for are chocolate syrup or cocoa mix, plastic bags, small toys, buttons, sharp bones, scissors, needles, pins, aluminum foil, and small light bulbs.

## Getting Ready to House-train

If your is to be litter-box-trained, place the box near its bed. When it awakes from a sleep, it will want to go to the potty right away.

If the pig is to be doggie-door-trained, be sure the path to the doggie door is clear of closed doors and other insurmountable obstacles.

## Food and Water Dishes

Have your pig's dishes for food and water ready. A good type of dish is a non-tip stainless-steel bowl. One can be used for water, and another for food. A two-quart bowl is a good size to use for each, although if your piglet is very small, you may have to start with smaller sizes. Because pigs like to sort through their food with their snouts, you need a bowl much larger than the amount of food you will offer at each meal. If you get bowls other than non-tip stainless, your pig will learn to root under it and flip it over to see if something better is underneath, so you will save yourself much grief and mopping if you use non-tip bowls from the start. If your pig becomes smart enough to figure out how to flip over the non-tip bowls, you may have to build a retainer for the bowls. However, a young pig that starts off with a non-tip bowl will see it cannot flip the bowl over and will continue believing this.

Remember, habits formed at an early age—either good or bad—are the hardest to change.

## Setting Up the Nursery

Try to pick a nursery location that will not make the pig feel isolated from the family but will nevertheless keep it confined to a particular area of the house. Full access to the house should be given gradually, *after* the pig has shown it is reliable about its toilet habits. If possible, pick a room that has exits you can barricade with see-through gates. This should be a room frequented by members of the family, because if the pig is isolated in a bathroom or utility room, it may become bored, frustrated, and lonesome. Think of your pig as an infant or toddler in need of both companionship and rules.

The nursery should contain the following:

1. A litter box that the pig can enter and turn around in easily. The size of the litter box should be increased as the pig grows. The bottom section of a travel crate for pets, with its existing door opening, works well. A small child's wading pool may be used, but for most pigs, especially very small ones, an entrance must be cut. Be sure to tape the edges or file them smooth, and round any corners so the pig does not injure itself. Wood shavings make ideal litter for the box. Avoid cat litter, which the pig will most likely taste and sometimes eat.

2. A bed your pig can call its own, with an old comforter, blankets, or towels. The top section of a travel crate works well, as do dog beds and baskets. You can be as elaborate as your decorating skills and pocketbook allow.

3. A few blankets and towels for your pig to root in and burrow under. Be sure they are washable.

4. A non-tip bowl for water. Always keep fresh water available.

5. A non-tip shallow food bowl that permits sorting through the food.

6. An assortment of playthings, such as balls, rawhide chew treats, plastic soda and milk bottles, old knotted socks, squeaky toys, and a stuffed animal or two.

If it is impossible to let your pig have access to a whole room, you can use a large child's playpen or a dog exercise pen as a substitute. But this does not give your pig much room, and may only teach the pig how to get along in confinement instead of teaching it to relieve itself outdoors. In addition, you will need to provide all the apparatus listed above, which will not give the pig much room to move around. If you must use this method, take the pig outside more frequently, and let it out to investigate the room when you feel confident that it will not have an "accident."

Letting your pig sleep in your bed is not recommended. Although this seems cute when the pig is small, a pig will become very pushy as an adult, and you may find yourself on the floor many nights.

## Outdoors

You may decide to train your pig as both an inside and outside pet. Providing outside access to a nice grazing area can be advantageous to both you and your pig. However, grave danger can be present in several forms outdoors.

First decide if your pig is to have access to the whole yard or if it will have a fenced-off area. To prevent your pig from rooting up your whole yard, consider penning off a small portion of the yard as a rooting area. Whenever your pig exhibits rooting behavior, direct it to the rooting area.

### Pig-proofing Your Yard

Check every bit of the area to which your pig has access for toxic plants. It is a matter of life and death that your yard have chemical-free grass for grazing. If you have fertilized or used pesticides, check the labels of these products for residual effects. Check the area for snail, roach, and mouse baits as well. If you have a barbecue, remove any charcoal or lighter fluid from the area. If there is a chance that *any* vehicle or lawn mower has been in the area, check for leaking gas, oil, and, most important, antifreeze. If you have any doubts about the toxicity of a substance or its residual effects on swine, consult "Poisoning" in this book, page 51, or call your county agent or veterinarian for advice.

### Protecting from Sun and Weather

Because pigs are highly susceptible to sunburn and heatstroke, adequate shade should

Provide a safe grazing area for your pig. Check all plants in the area that the pig has access to, against the list of toxic plants. Fruit trees are an invitation for your pig. They will eat fallen fruit as well as fruit from low branches and could become ill from overeating. Note also, that some leaves and pits are toxic.

be provided in a ventilated area. A roof put up in a corner of a wooden fence might provide shade, but without ventilation it could become very hot underneath on a sunny day. Natural shades such as trees and bushes are best, if possible. If your pig is uncomfortable, it will begin rooting to find a cool spot. If it gets too hot, it could perish.

Is there shelter available for the pig if there is rain, heavy winds, or cold weather? If possible, provide your pig with a little house where it can snuggle in a mound of hay during such weather.

### Access to Water

Indoors or outside, clear, fresh water should be provided for your pig. Some pig owners purchase a small child's wading pool for this purpose. If you buy one of these pools, it is

# *Bringing Your New Pig Home*

wise to make a wooden ramp or brick steps into and out of the pool. The pool should never be so full of water that the pig can drown. Add a few bricks as a resting place for the pig's head should it lie down. This water should be changed often, since pigs tend to urinate and sometimes defecate in the water. On hot, sunny days water can develop blue-green algae that may be toxic to your pig when consumed. Another thing to remember is that anything on your pig's skin (lotions, oils, etc.) will come off in the water and may prove dangerous if the pig drinks the water.

Do not let your pig have a "wallow," no matter how much you think it may enjoy one. Wallows are an invitation for your pig to defecate and urinate, and it can become a breeding place for infectious diseases and transmission of parasites. Some worm eggs live a very long time in water and wallows. Be sure the water you empty does not create a wallow for your pet.

## Setting Up the Outside Pen

A pig that has daily access to the outdoors will be healthier, happier, and less bored. In summary, there are several things to consider when setting up an outside home:
1. Be sure that all plants in the area are nontoxic. Even roses that have been treated with systemic insecticides can be harmful. Check to see that the area is free of vegetation that has been chemically treated in any way.
2. Check for electrical wires, sockets, and appliances.
3. Be sure the fence is secure enough to prevent the pig from going through it or rooting under it.
4. Provide a small house or pet travel crate as a place for your pig to sleep. Furnish it with dry hay or blankets.

When a pig is outdoors, it must be protected from the elements. Warm weather means protection from sun, heat, and drying wind; cold weather means protection from cold temperatures, rain, snow, and cold winds. Provide a properly fenced area with a well insulated house. Provide shade and a wading pool in hot weather.

5. Provide shelter from sun, heat, wind, rain, and cold.
6. Be sure no animals can enter the pen and harm or frighten your pig.

## Introducing Your Pig to Its New Home

If you are fortunate enough to have a pig who has been socialized and gentled by the breeder, you can skip this section. But if your pig is not gentle, follow these guidelines. Place the crate in which you brought it home, in a small, confined area. Open the door and let the pig come out gradually and check out its new surroundings. Remember, it has left everything and everyone it knew, it is vulner-

# Bringing Your New Pig Home

able, and it needs your kindness. When it appears less afraid, sit on the floor with the pig, and offer a treat from your hand. If the pig is frightened, move your hand slowly and deliberately in its direction. Do not make direct eye contact with the pig at this point. If you can touch the pig, scratch its chest and side with a gentle touch. Continue offering treats and scratching.

Repeat this process as often as you can during the day. If necessary, feed the total ration for several days in this manner, until it is forced to accept you and your attentions. Eventually, the pig will come to you. Talk to it in a reassuring voice. Do not make any fast moves or try to pick it up. Pigs resist being picked up and hugged. Eventually, however, most pigs love to sit on the lap of the person they live with. Each pig has a personality all its own. Some want to get close and touch their owners, while others prefer being more distant. Remember that most pigs really would like to be friendly, and respect their fears of being restrained and held up in the air.

Have both your nursery and outside pen prepared by the time you bring the pig home. Take your pig to its indoor area immediately and do not let it out unsupervised again until it is totally reliable in the house. After showing the pig its new litter box and bed, introduce it to its water bowl and its food bowl. The whole family should take time to socialize with the pig and make it feel welcome. Let it explore the territory inside for a few minutes, then pick it up and take it outside to its pen. If your pig runs away, further gentling is needed.

Walk beside your pig in a slow, nonthreatening manner and talk to it. By being in its small area, you will be socializing and litter-training it simultaneously. What you want is for the pig to trust you. Try to gain its confidence by sitting down on the floor with it, while talking to it. Coax it closer by offering it tidbits, scattering a few pieces close to you. The pig will gradually get close enough for you to touch it. When it does, very slowly move your hand under its chin and scratch it.

At this point, things should fall into place rapidly. Soon you will have your pig "eating out of your hand," both figuratively and literally. Call your pig by name from the time you bring it home. Pigs tend to bond tightly with the people of the household (their surrogate "herd members"), and are generally aloof and indifferent to visitors. Pigs hand-raised on bottles from a very early age tend to be friendly to all people, but could become biters as they mature.

# *When You Must Leave Home*

Caring for a pig is a lot like having a toddler in the house. You have to be concerned for its well-being and safety. When you must leave home, you have to do one of the following, depending on the length of time you will be gone:

- Take the pig with you.
- Leave it at home.
- Find someone to care for the pig.

## Have a Secure Place for Your Pig

If you decide to leave the pig at home, be sure you leave it in a place where it is protected from inclement weather and safe from anything that could hurt it. Remember, however, that a pig left alone can get into mischief, which can become learned behavior. That is, if the pig gets into trouble when you go out—by chewing something up it shouldn't, for instance—it is likely to repeat this behavior at another time. A pig that has been overhandled or has been constantly with its owner is particularly susceptible to becoming frustrated and can cause much damage. Confined in a small area, it might resort to destroying furniture, carpets, and even walls.

## Try to Find a Pig-sitter

Even so, there will no doubt be times when you will be away from home for some time and cannot take your pig with you. If your pig is an indoor/outdoor pig, with a pen of its own in the backyard, you may be able to leave it outside the entire time and have a neighbor look after it. Of course, a house-sitter with some pig experience is the ideal solution for an indoor pig. The pig will be happier in its own environment than if it is put outside. Introduce the pig and sitter in advance, and, if possible, have the sitter come to visit and feed the pig and learn its habits. Pigs do not like abrupt changes, and can become despondent and destructive if left alone for long periods.

## Boarding Your Pig

If you will be gone for a long time and it is not practical to enlist the services of a pig- or house-sitter, try to secure the help of friends or family members who can provide an environment in their home similar to one the pig presently enjoys.

Let this person take the pig overnight or over a weekend on a trial basis. This way, you can help monitor the behavior of your pet and you will feel more comfortable knowing what problems may arise when you are gone. Be sure you send along the pig's own bed, litter pan if the pig uses one, bowls and blankets, and any toys it likes. Pack your pig's daily ration of pellets in Ziploc bags. Your friends will probably want to overfeed your pig, since the pig will no doubt give them the "starving pig" look that melts even the coldest of hearts. Give your pig-sitters a complete list of allowable food items and amounts. Check to see if their house and yard are pig-proof, as you did your own yard and house when you brought your new pig home. Show them how the pig walks on a leash, enters a car, and the hazards connected with taking it along for a ride. Show them its tricks and tell them of its habits, good or bad.

Then give them this book to read and for reference, and the name of your veterinarian and other pig-smart people who can help handle medical or behavioral problems.

Be ready to fight to get your pig back when you return.

# *When You Must Leave Home*

## Traveling With Your Pig

Begin to take your pig for car rides early in its life. Riding in the car will soon become enjoyable for and relished by your pig. Be sure to have your pig harness-trained (see page 73) before you go for long rides so that you can stop to let the pig exercise and relieve itself. If you use public rest stops to exercise your pig on trips, be considerate and pick up all of its waste. Many rest stops have areas designated for pets. Wise pig owners remember that to some people, pigs are not pets but livestock. To save yourself much grief and avoid unpleasant encounters, always present your pig in its best light, as the neat, adorable little creature it is.

## Precautions

If you are taking your pig with you and you are planning to leave your car for any length of time, there are several points to consider:

You should *never* leave your pig alone in an unventilated car in warm weather. It can come down with heatstroke in a very short time. Remember, a closed car gets a lot hotter than the air outside, and you could return to find your pig has succumbed to the heat. If you leave the windows open, be sure they are closed to sufficient height so the pig cannot jump out. Another option is to take along a well-ventilated crate for your pig and leave the window open wider. Consider using the crate for the first few trips to see how it adjusts to the motion and new experience.

With your car properly ventilated for your pig's safety, there is the risk that someone will steal your car or its contents—including your pig. A good alarm system will warn you, if you are within earshot, when someone attempts to get into your car.

It is a good idea to take your pig along on car trips only if you will be remaining within sight and sound of the vehicle.

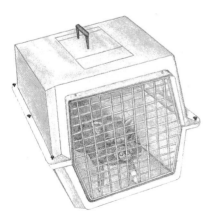

Teach your pig to accept temporary confinement in an airline crate. This will prove to be useful when you travel or have guests who do not wish to interact with your pig.

## Other Travel Considerations

Because your pet is so unusual and such a people-pleaser, it is fun taking it places. When it is small, you can lift it into your car or van, but as it grows, this will not be possible or practical. Instead, your pig should be taught to enter and leave the car without your help. If your car is low to the ground, you can start by building a small ramp of wood for the pig to climb.

Build a ramp from the ground to the bottom of the car-door opening that is of such a length that it has a gradual slope. Be sure the ramp has cross treads and carpet for traction. It should be designed in such a way that it will not slip away from the car.

Before attaching the ramp to the car, train

your pig on the ramp away from the car. Place the ramp on your lawn, on indoor carpet, propped up on one end by a brick and with one side of the ramp along a wall, if possible. Stand along the other edge to prevent the pig from stepping off the side. Put a small trail of treats along the center of the ramp. Tell the pig "Go up." When the pig is negotiating the board perfectly, put the end of the board on a low step and repeat the process. When the pig reaches the other end of the board, it will have somewhere to go: up. Use the same principle for teaching the pig to go down the ramp.

When the pig appears comfortable with this height, put the end of the board on the next-highest step and repeat the lesson. Mastery of this level should make the pig ready for entering the car.

## Entering the Car

Put the ramp in position. Ask an assistant to open the door on the opposite side of the car, and hand the pig's leash to that person. *Gently*, coaxing with treats in your hand or on the ramp itself, urge your pig to start up the ramp with *very light* pressure on the leash. Give the pig a verbal command, such as "Up", or "Get in." Use simple words and use them consistently. It may take several days for the pig to accomplish this feat.

As the pig gets larger, you may find that it no longer needs the ramp and that at a simple verbal command it will leap into the car with no assistance. Once the pig has entered the car, praise it for this accomplishment, let it rest, and show it the way down the ramp. Make car riding a fun experience for your pig and it will delight at the jingle of your car keys.

The back seat is safer for your pig than the front seat. Although your pig can be taught to be restrained with a seat belt, the car's heat

Use a ramp with cross treads to teach your pig to enter the car. Begin with placing the ramp on the ground with one end on a brick. Make a trail of treats up the ramp. Stand next to the ramp so the pig cannot get the treats without actually walking on the ramp. When the pig has mastered the ramp on the brick, teach it to walk up the ramp to the car. Many pigs eventually learn to enter the car without the ramp.

and air conditioning may blow directly upon it and cause health problems. Also, if you have to stop suddenly, your pig could be thrown through your windshield if it is not strapped in. Also, if the pig became stressed for any reason, it could try to climb into the driver's lap and cause an accident.

Be sure your pig has relieved itself before you leave on any trip, no matter how short. One or two mishaps in your car, and you will need an industrial-strength car freshener.

Every owner of a pet pig should follow a sensible health program to keep the pig fit and happy. Several factors contribute to the pig's general well-being:
- Diet and nutrition
- Environment and protection from the elements

# Feeding Your Pig Properly

- Exercise
- Vaccinations and immunizations
- Attention to grooming, including feet and teeth
- Daily monitoring of the pig's condition

Preventing a disease is much easier than treating an infected animal, so follow your veterinarian's immunization and vaccination schedule to the letter. Never expose your pig to other pigs that are not on the same program you are following.

Check your pig every day. If you discover a health problem early, you may be in time to save your pig's life. The problem could be very complex, or as simple as a cold floor or draft. Remember, your veterinarian is trained to recognize symptoms and their causes, so don't try to diagnose or treat health problems yourself.

Finally, use the following guidelines for your pet's diet. Nutrition is a key factor in keeping a miniature pig healthy.

## Water

Newborn pigs are about 90 percent water. As they grow older, about 70 percent of their body is water. Water is contained in the body cells, the lymph system, joint fluid, blood, and other body fluids. Every day, the pig loses water through its urine, feces, respiration, evaporation from the skin, and sweating.

Water is necessary to dissolve nutrients so that they can be absorbed by the body. Water-soluble wastes are eliminated from the body as urine and sweat. Solid wastes are softened by water in the digestive tract before they are eliminated. All of the pig's body fluids, such as blood, gastric juices, and lymph, joint and peritoneal fluids, are dependent on a proper water balance.

Water is also needed to maintain proper body temperature. Because it is a good conductor for heat, it can transfer heat from the internal body to the skin surface, which permits heat loss.

If the pig is left for even a short time without the proper water balance in hot temperatures, dehydration, resulting in stress and even death, may occur.

Most of the water that is lost by the body must be replenished, or the pig will become dehydrated. This water is replaced mainly by drinking. Water is also found in all foodstuffs, even grains and pellets that look dry. A pig will drink between 7 and 20 percent of its body weight in water each day. The amount of water needed is determined by several factors:

- Amount of water loss in the pig during a given period
- Temperature and humidity
- Age of the pig
- Health of the pig
- Activity level of the pig
- Moisture content of any food consumed
- Protection from sun and wind

Provide your pig with fresh, clean water at all times. It is better to use small containers that the pig cannot climb into. Clean water containers daily. Keep outside water containers out of direct sunlight if possible, so they will not be contaminated with blue-green algae. This microscopic plant can become visible in your pig's water within 24 hours if the temperature and sunlight are favorable. It does not grow as rapidly in partial sunlight or shade. Be sure the water cannot become con-

Top: Fred-Rec Von Pig has a house when he is outdoors to protect him from the elements. Tabatha likes her bed in the house filled with blankets.
Bottom: Introduce your pig to bathing at an early age by using a wading pool with just a few inches of water. Here Tabatha is introduced to the pool, and Oscar is scrubbed into ecstasy.

# *Feeding Your Pig Properly*

taminated with feces or urine from the pig or other animals. If you ever need to increase the water consumption of your pig, offer it at a warm temperature. Pigs prefer tepid water to cold water even in very warm weather.

## Nutrition

The size of your pig is determined by two things: nutrition and genetics. You cannot change the genetics of your pig by depriving it of adequate nourishment, but you can cause a genetically small pig to grow excessively.

It is fun to watch a pig eat, because it devours all food with such gusto. Pigs make even the worst cook feel like a real gourmet, because they enjoy food, and a lot of it. But many a pet pig has had its life shortened by a well-meaning but uninformed owner who overfeeds the pig. Overfeeding will create an obese pig that can develop joint, leg, foot, and other health problems. Remember, you are not producing *pork*, you are maintaining a pet.

Think about the size of a pig's leg bones, the surface area of the foot, and the weight it carries compared to human equivalents. A pig of normal weight carries about double the weight per square inch of foot as does a human of normal weight. An overweight pig will put undue stress on these bones and joints, which can cause chronic arthritis and joint disease.

House pigs will become relentless beggars if you begin to feed them between meals. Never feed your pig from the refrigerator.

Top: Olivia demonstrates that nose tricks such as "making a touchdown" or "ring toss" are fun to teach your miniature pig.
Bottom: A miniature pig can quickly learn to "run the barrels" or "thread the needle" by using a tasty treat to guide its path.

When it becomes hungry, it will remember where it was satisfied. It will nudge the refrigerator, and soon the nudges will become strong rooting action that may open the door. You may return home to a pig in "hog heaven," smack in the middle of the total contents of your refrigerator, with an even fatter tummy and a smug smile on its face.

## How to Keep Your Pig Satisfied and Healthy

If you were growing a pig for market, you would put it on full feed. However, a pet pig should remain on a regular feed schedule. Do not feed your pig between meals except for training treats, and then reduce the normal food ration by an amount equal to the quantity used in training, taking the extra exercise into consideration.

Your pig's food should be:
- High quality
- High fiber
- High volume
- Low calorie

A pelleted feed especially formulated for miniature pigs is available in some areas. If you are unable to obtain this food, you can substitute other feeds. Advanced technology has created some foods that are designed to create rapid and large growth. These foods are not recommended for miniature pigs.

### Components of Pig Food

The food your pig consumes should contain the following components:

**Protein and Amino Acids:** This ingredient is necessary to produce muscle and growth. A pig fed too little protein can carry more body fat. Amino acids must be present in the diet so the body can properly use the protein. The

# *Feeding Your Pig Properly*

Provide the pig with an adequate grazing area or a few handfuls of alfalfa hay along with the regular ration of pig pellets. If neither hay nor grazing are available, alfalfa pellets can be used instead.

protein found in corn and soybeans is superior to animal protein sources for the pig.

**Fat:** A pig must have at least 1 to 2 percent fat in its diet. Too much fat in the diet will cause an overweight pig. Too little fat in the diet will cause loss of hair, scaling skin, and an unthrifty pig. A pregnant and lactating sow needs a greater proportion of fat in her diet.

**Minerals:** Many minerals are essential in a pig's diet. Some interact with each other and are necessary in proper levels to prevent deficiencies. Calcium and phosphorus are two important minerals that work together and are important in the pig's skeletal growth. Other necessary minerals are sodium chloride (salt), iodine, iron, copper, cobalt, manganese, potassium, magnesium, zinc, and selenium. Selenium, a necessary mineral in miniature swine, is discussed under "How to Feed," page 000. Grass for grazing, hay, and crops growing in some areas west of the Mississippi are generally selenium-deficient.

**Vitamins:** Vitamins are required by swine in varying amounts according to age, activity, and use as breeding animals. Those vitamins are: vitamins A, B, (thiamin, riboflavin, niacin, pantothenic acid, pyridoxine, cyanocobocanine [B-12], biotin, folic acid), C (ascorbic acid), D, E, and K. Swine can syn-

thesize vitamin C, so it rarely has to be added to their daily ration.

## Parts of a Basic Diet

A basic diet for a pet pig should contain several basic elements.

Whenever possible, provide your pig with unlimited grazing on chemical-free grass. If this is not possible, furnish it with a high-quality hay such as alfalfa or oat. This roughage is very important, but feed within reason!

Fifty percent of the balance of the diet should be a good-quality commercial pig food. There are pelleted foods on the market specifically for miniature pigs. Feed pig starter to pigs under two months, and adult food to all others. Since you are not planning to send your pig to market, do not use pig grower or finisher. Much research has gone into developing these foods that are designed to put on weight and bulk, neither of which is desirable for a pet pig. If your pig is a gilt or sow that is pregnant or lactating, there is a commercially available ration specifically for her. Pig starter is normally 15 percent protein, 4 percent fat, and at least 4 percent fiber. Adult rations are usually 15 percent protein, 3 percent fat, and at least 5 percent fiber. These foods may be

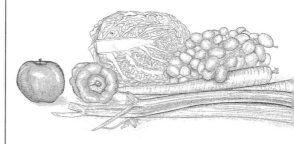

Fresh fruits and vegetables include your salad trimmings. A variety, in moderation, will help your pig to be satisfied and healthy.

# Feeding Your Pig Properly

medicated or nonmedicated. What this means is that a specific medication, often an antibiotic, is added to the food before it is pelletized. This antibiotic is added to prevent and control certain gastrointestinal diseases, but its inclusion in the diet produces the side effect of weight gain. This gain can be as much as 15 percent of the pig's weight. Before considering a medicated feed, remember: only certain diseases respond to the antibiotic, and it is not a replacement for routine health management.

Pelleted pig food is partly made up of by-products from the manufacture of food and drink for humans and other animals. The main ingredients in most pelleted feeds are:

**Grain Products, Processed Grain By-products, and Plant Protein Products:** These first three ingredients usually are found in barley, wheat, corn, milo, oats, sugar beet pulp, cottonseed meal, linseed meal, soybean meal, peanut meal, safflower meal, cull beans, distiller's by-products, brewer's by-products, millings, and screenings from granaries.

**Animal Protein Products:** These are usually found in by-products of the meat and fish industries, such as fish and poultry meal.

**Added Vitamin Supplements:** Vitamins A, D, E, and B are found in alfalfa meal, brewer's yeast, peanut meal, animal by-products, fish meal, soybean meal, liver meal, milk products, and rice polishings.

**Added Mineral Supplements:** Calcium (in several forms found in bone meal, limestone, and oyster shell) salt, manganese oxide, zinc oxide, copper sulfate, ferrous sulfate, and cobalt sulfate.

Twenty-five percent of the pig's diet can consist of fruits and vegetables.; Be sure all vegetables are thoroughly washed to remove any possible chemicals, such as insecticides, preservatives, and waxes. Some vegetables can be fed in larger quantities if they are low in calories; these include cucumbers, celery, lettuce, bell peppers, cabbage, broccoli, and green beans. Pigs find delicious many vegetable parts that we normally throw away. Keep a plastic container in your refrigerator to hold peelings and cores of cabbage, lettuce, apples, melons, tomatoes, eggplant, bell peppers, potatoes, squash, and carrots. Feed the starchy vegetables with discretion. Pigs love banana peels, but do not feed citrus peels. Other fruits and vegetables pigs love are: bananas, peaches, pears, melons, corn (feed sparingly), tomatoes, eggplant, boiled onions, plums, and peeled citrus. Good training treats are apples, grapes, raisins, frozen peas, and raw peanuts.

To provide bulk, up to 25 percent of the pig's diet can be bran. Never give bran when the pig is under oral medication, because the medication will pass through the pig's system too rapidly. If you see puddinglike stools, bran should be omitted or reduced until the condition is corrected. Some pigs may be sensitive to bran at a young age.

## How Much to Feed

Several factors determine the amount of food to feed your pet pig:
- The age of the pig
- The pig's individual metabolic rate
- The pig's level of activity and exercise
- The pig's current body condition

Use good judgment, and watch your pig's condition. If you are feeding the recommended diet and your pig gains weight, reduce the amount of feed. If it appears too thin, increase the feed. The following chart shows a basic, complete, well-rounded diet for the average pig; you may wish to consider it for your miniature pig. Based on the needs of an average-sized potbelly pig, the ration averages out to one-half cup per 25 pounds of body

# Feeding Your Pig Properly

weight. The amounts are "per day" and should be divided into two equal feedings.

| Age | Boars and pets | Breeder Females |
|---|---|---|
| 6 to 10 weeks | ½ to 1 cup | ½ to 1 cup |
| 10 to 14 weeks | 1 cup to 1¼ cups | 1 to ½ cups |
| 14 weeks to 6 months | 1¼ to 2 cups | 1½ to 2 ½ cups |
| 6 months and over | 2 to 2½ cups | 3 to 3½ cups |

## How to Feed

Use a no-tip bowl. Feed your pig its pellets and bran first. Most pigs love the taste of the pellets. They will root around in the bowl trying to find them, knocking the rest of the food out of the bowl. When the pig is finished with the pellets and bran, add the vegetables a few at a time. If the bowl is large enough, you can feed both vegetables and pig pellets, allowing for some rooting behavior.

Feed at the same time each day, and remember not to feed between meals. Never, ever, feed the pig while you are eating, or it will become an obnoxious pest and make a complete pig of itself! This habit is very hard to break, so don't let your friends talk you into letting them give your pig a piece of their cookie or sandwich. When your pig is an adult, you will not enjoy its little hard hooves on your legs or its nose nudging you until you have a black-and-blue ankle.

If your pig is bored, you can scatter pelleted food and let the pig take some time finding and eating it. More is *not* better. Oversupplementation can cause toxic reactions and chemical imbalances in your pig that could be more severe than a deficiency. Feed your pig a well-balanced diet and check with your vet to see if you should add a vitamin-mineral supplement.

A mineral important to your pig's health is selenium. This mineral occurs naturally in the soil in many parts of this country, but there are also areas that are extremely deficient in this mineral. Pigs that have free access to grazing and rooting in soil in a nondeficient area will not need additional selenium. If your pig is a house pet and rarely has time to root in the soil, you will need to add selenium to its diet. Companies that specialize in making the vitamins for livestock and exotic animal breeders usually offer a choice of rations with added selenium or without added selenium. Too much can be harmful to your pig, so before using a supplement with selenium added check with your county agent (if your pig has outside access) to see what the status of this mineral is in your area. In many areas, you can get a soil test kit, collect a sample, and mail it with a small fee for a laboratory report on your soil's chemical composition. Generally, soil west of the Mississippi is selenium-deficient, while soil east of the Mississippi is not.

Pigs are born iron-deficient and need an iron supplement soon after birth. Older pigs get enough iron from their daily ration.

There are additives for your pig's food to enhance its skin and hair coat and deodorize musky-smelling boars. Read the label to see exactly what an additive should do for your pig, and be sure to offer the amount recommended. The hair and skin conditioner may be high in fat and calories, and overfeeding will cause unwanted weight gain. If you want to improve skin and hair coat without an additive, try using a tablespoon of corn oil or safflower oil with your pig's daily ration. *Do not feed animal fats!*

# *Grooming Your Pig*

## Teeth

Dental care is becoming more accepted among pet owners. Most pigs do not like their teeth brushed, but you can use a small washcloth with baking soda or toothpaste on it to rub its teeth. Be careful, so that you are not bitten. Try, when your pig is small, to introduce regular toothbrushing. Several times weekly is sufficient if the pig is on a normal diet that does not contain much refined sugar, which causes tooth decay in pigs and people.

**Needle Teeth:** There are eight needle teeth or eyeteeth that should be shortened 12 to 24 hours after the pig's birth, by clipping. This will save the mother and littermates from unnecessary injury due to the newborns' nipping with these sharp teeth. Either cuticle scissors or small electrician's wire nippers can be used. Hold the pig's mouth open with a flat carpenter's pencil or soft kitchen spatula and clip the teeth close to the gum line. If you do not clip these teeth short enough, the pigs will chew on each other's ears relentlessly and cause injury to the mother's teats. Using this method, clipping the teeth takes only a minute or two and causes minimal stress to the piglets.

**Tusks:** The canines in the boar develop into tusks between two and three years of age, but begin around a year in miniature pigs. (In altered males and sows, the tusks normally do not grow any longer than regular teeth.) They continue to grow for the life of the boar. They are the top and bottom canines, and both have curved upward by the time a pig reaches maturity. Sometimes these tusks will wear down or break off; however, this is not likely, and you should consider having them removed or sawed off by a veterinarian to prevent problems.

The boar can be secured by using two nooses over its snout. If excessive straining occurs, anesthesia may be necessary. The boar will rub the tusks together when he is excited, flattening the touching surfaces and honing them to knifelike sharpness. When handling a boar, a quick movement of its head against your leg or arm can cause a serious gash. With gentle miniature pigs there is rarely a problem, but if the pig is excited, agitated, injured, or ill, the behavior can be unpredictable.

**Regular tooth care:** Periodic checking of your pig's teeth can show if a problem has occurred, such as a broken tooth, abscess, or residual tartar buildup. Teeth can be scaled with dental tools. This procedure is not difficult, but getting the pig to cooperate is. If buildup is such that a long time is required to clean the teeth, a tranquilizer or anesthetic may be required.

## Bathing

Pigs love to be groomed, whether it be washing, bathing, brushing and scratching, applying lotion to the skin, or ear cleaning.

Pigs by nature love water, and they should be introduced to having baths at an early age. Very young pigs and small pigs can be bathed in the bathtub. Put a nonslip carpet or towel in the bottom. Be sure the water is not cold the first time. Put only one or two inches of warm water in the tub and a few pieces of vegetables in the water. Leaves from lettuce or celery will float and get your pig's attention. Slowly lift the pig into the tub of water, taking care that the animal does not slip. If it does not notice the floating leaves, pick one up and offer it at water level, then watch the pig figure out this new adventure. The first few minutes, just let it eat the treats while standing in the water. Then, using a small brush or sponge with a handle, begin to massage its skin. Pay

# *Grooming Your Pig*

The easiest way to bathe your pig is to use a small child's wading pool. Begin by floating some leaves of lettuce in the water to distract the pig. Take your time and be patient. Your pig will soon love this attention.

special attention to the pig's hooves and tummy. A sponge with a hollow handle that can hold shampoo is an excellent tool for bathing your pig. If you plan to use the food method when washing your pig, put the food in a colander with small legs after the pig gets used to it; the soapy water will drain out the bottom. A word of warning: many pigs defecate while being bathed, so don't think your pig is unusual if this happens.

As your pig gets larger, or whenever the weather is warm, switch to a child's wading pool outside for its bath. Begin with the smallest one you can buy, putting just a few inches of warm water in it. Gradually introduce a water hose and cooler water with a stiffer brush. A soft spray nozzle for watering flowers may be helpful for rinsing. While the pig is still wet, apply a fine spray of moisturizing oil to its skin. There are several commercially available bath oils that can be applied in this way. Rub the oil in the pig's coat, and pat dry. Remember not to leave the pig oily, or the oil

will rub off on everything it touches, including your furniture and your pant legs. I recommend Keri Lotion or Avon Skin-So-Soft bath oils. They will make your pig look, feel, and smell wonderful. Avon Skin-So-Soft has the additional effect of repelling skin pests.

Gear your bathing schedule to the condition of your pig's skin and its own natural cleanliness. Overbathing can cause excessively dry and flaky skin.

## Cleaning Ears

Ear cleaning; is something that pigs love. To them it is another form of rubbing and scratching. If your pig has contact with other animals, regularly check its ears for ear mites, which are as common with pigs as with dogs and cats. There are preparations specifically for ear mites and a topical pour-on insecticide that will rid your pig of all external pests. Ask

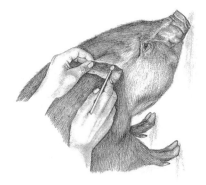

Routinely check your pig's ears for infections and mites. Clean the ears with cotton swabs and rubbing alcohol. If the cotton swab has a foul odor, it is probably an indication of ear mite infestation or infection.

your veterinarian about them. When cleaning your pig's ears, use a washcloth and cotton swabs dipped in rubbing alcohol. If you get water in its ears, you may create an environment conducive to ear infection. Use extreme caution when cleaning the ear with cotton swabs, because the pig may make a sudden movement that results in injury.

## Foot Care

The pig's hoof is a very interesting adaptation of nature. Unlike the cow's and horse's, it does not have a hard bottom. It is more like four soft toes, each surrounded on the sides and front by a strong "nail." If the pig lives indoors, it will not get enough wear on its foot to keep the nail portion short, and the soft portion will not have thick skin. As a consequence, house pigs can sustain injury to their feet by stepping on nails, glass, sharp stones, and the like.

Begin when the pig is young, by handling its feet when it is lying down, and eventually pretending to put a small amount of pressure on the "nail" portion as if you were clipping it. It will need very little trimming when the pig is a youngster, but as the pig gets older and heavier, you will need to keep its feet properly trimmed so it can distribute its weight in a way that will not be harmful to its legs. A pig with overgrown hooves can become knock-kneed and splay-footed, and have weak pasterns. See the conformation diagram for location of this area.

An easy way to keep the hooves trimmed is with a pony hoof nipper and large file. You can also use an emery board or sandpaper stapled to a block of wood. Let the pig play "dead hog" and fall over while you are scratching its tummy. After you have it relaxed, you can carefully manipulate its feet and get it used to the feel. Your pig will then probably let you do some clipping on its hooves and allow some filing. This will most likely take you several applications, but it is well worth the effort when the task is completed.

Because the outside of the pig's hoof is like a thick fingernail surrounding the meaty, tender toe, be extremely careful not to cut the toe.

Hoof conditioners for horses can be used on pigs to keep their hooves in top condition.

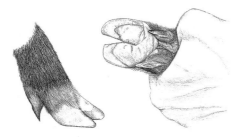

The pig's foot consists of two meaty toes, each surrounded by a thick "nail" and two smaller, but similar dew claws higher up on the leg.

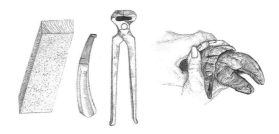

The pig's hooves and dew claws must be trimmed to keep the feet and leg structures healthy. A small pair of pony nippers or hoof knive may be used in extreme cases such as the overgrown hoof in this drawing. Emery boards or sandpaper stapled to a block of wood can be used to file hooves in good condition that are not overgrown.

# Disease Prevention and Control

The most effective means of preventing and controlling swine disease are the following:

Eliminate and prevent diseases by keeping a closed herd. If you have a single pig, keep it away from other pigs unless you are sure that they are cared for with the same techniques that you use (vaccinations and keeping them away from other pigs). Vaccinate for those diseases that have vaccines available. Maintain good sanitation. Purchase and keep stock only from validated disease-free herds.

Pigs are sensitive to many different organisms (bacterial, fungal, and viral) that can cause disease. Most of these organisms are different from those that cause disease in dogs and cats. Many of these diseases may be prevented, controlled, and treated with:

- Discriminatory contact with other pigs
- Constant awareness of and attention to environmental conditions
- A sound vaccination/immunization program
- Appropriate antibiotic therapy
- Regularly checking your pig for injuries and disease
- A well-planned means of internal and external parasite control

## Discriminatory Contact with Other Pigs

One way breeders of swine reduce the incidence of disease in their herd is to limit or totally eliminate contact with swine outside their herd. This is called maintaining a "semi-closed" or "closed" compound. All animals are specifically chosen from disease-free herds. All new or returning animals are quarantined for 30 to 60 days, in total isolation from any other animal on the premises. The animal's health is closely monitored. All persons who leave the compound undergo disinfecting procedures upon returning. All new animals are thoroughly tested before leaving quarantine. Sanitation is kept at a high level to prevent animal-to-animal or animal-to-man-to-animal contamination. Introduction of diseases and parasites is thereby kept to a minimum.

You can benefit from this method of disease control by greatly reducing the contact of your pig with outside pigs. If your pig contacts another pig or group of pigs, it has, in reality, come in contact with all the pigs those other pigs have been in contact with for the past few weeks. Do not be afraid to be fussy when choosing your pig's friends.

If you enter your pig in a show or training class where it is to be in contact with other pigs, be certain its vaccination program is complete for the area in which you live. Keep it away from other pig's fecal matter. Parasite eggs and bacteria can be carried on its feet, and later rubbed off in its own area at home. If possible, avoid body contact between pigs at these events.

Never feed or water your pig from pans or dishes that are not its own. If you are taking your pig where it will need to be fed or watered, take its equipment with you, and disinfect it when you bring the pig home. If your pig will be spending the night, take its bed or crate along also.

## Attention to Environmental Conditions

Sensible monitoring of the pig's daily living conditions can help reduce the incidence of some diseases and disorders. Pigs are highly susceptible to upper-respiratory diseases and arthritic disorders. Keep your pig in an environment that is free of cold, damp, and hard flooring to reduce the possibility of joint diseases. These conditions can increase the possibility of illness due to respiratory diseases.

In warm weather, pigs must be protected from excessive sun and heat to prevent sunburn and heatstroke. Provide adequately shaded, well-ventilated areas for your pig when it is out of doors.

## Checking Your Pig for Injuries and Disease

A properly vaccinated pig may become ill from a disease for which it could not be vaccinated. Watch for signs of illness or distress, such as weaving, head shaking, head nodding, pacing, pawing, self-mutilation, tail chewing or rubbing, unusual chewing behavior, eating feces, excessive drinking, lethargy, depression, anxious behavior, sitting up in a dog-type position, diarrhea, lack of bowel movement, loss of appetite, eating of unusual items, and so on. In other words, any deviation from your pig's normal behavior may be a warning sign that something wrong is going on in its body or its environment. Contact your veterinarian if any of the above, or other unusual behavior, is observed.

**Abscesses and Cuts:** Although a pig's skin is extremely tough, any break in it can result in invasion by bacteria that cause abscesses. These skin breaks may be caused by hypodermic injections, bites, cuts, and slivers. Proper sanitation measures should be practiced when giving injections of any type. Treatment by antibiotic is effective if you know the identity of the invading bacteria. If lancing of abscesses becomes necessary, this should be attempted only by a veterinarian.

## Know Your Pig's Normal Metabolic Rates

**Normal heart rate, pulse, temperature**
- The normal pulse for your pig is 58–86 per minute.
- Temperature 102–103.6 degrees F (38.8°–39.8°C).
- Respiration 10–20 per minute.

Keep a record of your pig's health history and a diary of its normal behavior. To find a "normal" temperature, check it at the same time each day. A temperature taken when a pig is just waking up will be lower than one taken later in the day, when the pig has been up awhile and been moving about and eating. One pig may run a normal temperature one degree more or less than another pig. For example, your pig may have a normal temperature of 102.0 (38.8°C), while another may have a normal temperature of 103.5 (39.7°C). If you suspect that your pig might be ill and its temperature is 103. 5 (39.7°C), you will know your pig is sick. If the pig hasn't been excited or stressed by some external stimuli, it might have a bacterial or viral infection.

**How to Take the Pig's Temperature:** If you have trained your pig well, it should behave nicely on an examination table. If your pig is very large, you may have to take its temperature with the pig standing on the floor. The pig's temperature can only be taken rectally. If you give it a special treat it likes, and it may not even notice you slipping the lubricated thermometer in its rectum. Since a pig's nose takes precedence over nearly everything else in its life, keep its front end busy while you work with its rear end. It is very important that you take the temperature when the pig is calm and not agitated. A fighting pig's temperature probably will be elevated from its struggling, and you will not know if it has a fever or not.

A digital thermometer works very well with pigs, because it registers the temperature faster; many are designed to beep when the temperature registers.

A pig's normal temperature is between 101.6 and 103.6 degrees Fahrenheit (38.8°–39.8°C). If there is any deviation from this, a health problem may exist, especially if you see other symptoms. It is time to check with your veterinarian.

## The Veterinarian: Your Pet's Second Best Friend

### Choosing Your Veterinarian

Many veterinarians specialize in particular species of animals. A veterinarian specializing in dogs and cats may not have the experience and expertise to treat pet pigs, or may wish not to treat pigs at all. The immunizations and medicines your pet needs are specifically for pigs, and a veterinarian may not have them available. If you live in a rural area, finding a competent veterinarian who can and will treat pet swine is usually not difficult. Many country veterinarians develop their practices around both large and small animals and will have the necessary medications and expertise for treating your pig. Though your pig is a pet, many of its health considerations, especially diseases, are similar to those of commercial swine. Once you have found a veterinarian that can and will treat pet pigs, ask for an immunization schedule that is best for your area. Certain areas of the country have diseases that are more prevalent at varying times of the year. In fact, proximity to commercial hog owners can have a direct ef-

fect on the type of program your veterinarian will help develop for you.

It is extremely important to develop a rapport with your veterinarian because he or she can be your best ally in the care of your pig.

### Getting Ready to Visit Your Veterinarian

You should know something about your pig's medical needs before visiting your veterinarian. Do not skimp on vaccinations, immunizations, and deworming just because your pig is not exposed to other pigs. Some diseases are airborne or transmitted via soil. Other diseases or parasites are transmitted by intermediate carriers, or "fomites," such as clothing, shoes, or other pets. Certain rodents and insects can be vectors of parasites or diseases.

It is important that your pig is socialized properly before you take it to the veterinarian, because it is difficult if not impossible for a veterinarian to examine a screaming and ill-mannered pig. If your pig is not trained properly, you may be wasting a trip, your veterinarian's time, and the cost of an office call.

### Training Your Pig Before It Goes to the Veterinarian

Begin training your pig at home, when it is very young, to stand on a small grooming table. Put a piece of nonslip carpet on top of the table to give the pig good footing. It is important that your pig's experiences on the table are positive and not frightening. Be slow, deliberate, and gentle when it is placed on the table. Have a pocket full of treats to reward the pig if it is calm and cooperative. Do not discipline your pig if it is afraid of the height or new surface; instead, place the piece of carpet on a much lower platform and try your pig at that height. Gently brush the pig and scratch it above the tail and on the back. Try not to scratch its side, or it may fall over or off the table. Do this only for a short time, unless the pig is having fun. Increase the time period each time you practice. Your veterinarian will be very grateful to you and pleased with your pig if it permits an examination without a fuss. You, too, may be thankful that you trained your pig to behave on an examination table, because someday you may find yourself in a predicament where you have to take its temperature or examine it.

## Introducing Your Pig to the Veterinarian

It is important that your pig's first visit to the veterinarian be a positive one. Pigs have strong memories, so make your first visit fun. Take your pig to the veterinarian for a checkup when it is young. Saving part of the morning's food ration for the veterinarian to offer will make a lasting impression in the pig's mind that the vet's is a good place to be. Also, take a handful of raisins or other treat for when it behaves like a good patient.

Ask your veterinarian if he or she can use the smallest-gauge needle he has for any vaccinations or immunizations. At a young age, your pig has very soft skin just behind its ears and on the inside of its thighs that will permit

Teach your pig when it is a baby to stand for examination on a small table. Your veterinarian will appreciate your efforts and will be better able to examine your calm pig.

entry of even a 25-gauge tuberculin syringe. The smallest needle used by most veterinarians is 23-gauge, which will cause a bit more discomfort than the 25-gauge. As the pig gets older, the gauge of the needle must be heavier to penetrate the thicker skin that comes with age and exposure to the elements.

Before you go to the veterinarian the first time, read the section on restraining your pig for medication and treatment. Practice the methods discussed there as much as you can. Remember to give a treat only if the pig stops screaming and fighting.

## Infectious Diseases

The following is a list and brief description of most swine diseases and a discussion of any available vaccine.

### Gastrointestinal

**Transmittable Gastroenteritis (TGE):** This common small-intestine disease can wipe out an entire litter. The virus causes starvation and

Teach your pig at an early age to be held in the manner illustrated. When being held in this position, you can scratch its tummy with one thumb. Most pigs taught this position at an early age enjoy it and submit readily. Your veterinarian will be able to utilize this position when blood withdrawal is necessary for certain tests.

# Disease Prevention and Control

dehydration by destroying digestive-tract cells. Incubation is about 18 hours, and progression is rapid. TGE is spread by bodily contact or in the air. There is a vaccine that can be given to pregnant sows two to four weeks before farrowing that will provide passive TGE immunity in the offspring. Provide a warm, draft-free environment for the baby pigs, with adequate water to prevent dehydration. This disease is mostly found in nursing and weaner pigs, but older pigs can also contract it. A recovered pig can shed the virus for over four months.

*Clostridium perfringens* **Type C Enteritis:** This highly fatal disease of the small intestine affects piglets one or two days old. The disease is preventable by vaccinating pregnant sows, who then pass on the immunity to fetuses via colostrum, or first milk.

*Enteric colibacillosis* **(*E. Coli*):** This disease is often called "white scours." Sows can be vaccinated for the disease and provide passive immunity to their offspring. This intestinal disorder is characterized by profuse amounts of yellowish, foul-smelling, watery diarrhea, dehydration, and commonly, death. Treatment is possible with antibacterial drugs and fluid therapy. Prevention is achieved by keeping quarters clean, dry, and warm, and by providing adequate milk from mother or bottle.

**Swine Dysentery (Bloody Scours):** This disease, which affects the large intestine, is characterized by loose stools followed by those that contain blood and mucus, usually in 8–14-week-old pigs. Dehydration, weakness, and emaciation result. There is no vaccine, but the disease can be controlled if treated early with antibiotics, which can be placed in the water.

**Rotaviral Enteritis (White or Milk Scours):** This is a common disease of the small intestine in pigs of all ages, but mostly in nursing and weaner pigs. Although death from the disease is rare, pigs must get adequate colostrum and milk, and be kept dry and warm.

**Swine Coccidiosis:** Referred to as "baby pig scours," this disease is prevalent in pigs seven to ten days old. Piglets will be weak, dehydrated, and undersize, and have diarrhea. Anticoccidial drugs administered to sows two weeks before farrowing may help in prevention, but disinfection and feces removal is absolutely imperative.

## Respiratory Diseases

**Atrophic Rhinitis:** Vaccines are available for this disease, which inflames the mucous membranes in the pig's nose. The bone in the nose can waste away or fail to develop properly, causing twisting or deviation deformity of the nose. Carriers of the disease are rodents, dogs, and cats. Symptoms include sneezing and a deformed, wrinkled nose in young pigs.

**Mycoplasmal Pneumonia (Swine Enzootic Pneumonia, SEP):** This disease is chronic and affects pigs of all ages. A dry cough and growth retardation are symptoms. Antibiotics can be used to treat the symptoms, but the only sure method of control is to buy stock from disease-free herds.

**Necrotic Rhinitis (Bull-Nose):** An uncommon disease of young pigs affecting the mucous membranes of the nose or mouth, usually due to an injury. Clipping needle teeth too short will cause damage to the roof of the mouth and permit entry of organisms.

**Pasteurellosis:** This disease is a complication of mycoplasmal pneumonia. It occurs in piglets and has even been found in aborted fetuses. Early antibiotic therapy is necessary to prevent chronic infection.

**Swine Influenza:** This acute, highly infectious disease is caused by a very common virus that raises body temperature and causes muscle soreness and "superinfection" by bacteria. If it is diagnosed early and treated with antibiotics, there should be low death loss. If not treated, it can become permanently epidemic in a herd. Inactivated influenza vaccines are available in some areas.

***Haemophilus Pleuropneumonia* (HPP):** A severe and highly contagious bacteria-caused pneumonia, primarily in pigs under six months of age. Although it can be treated with various drugs, survivors often remain carriers, making control difficult. Vaccines are available.

## Arthritic Diseases

**Erysipelas:** Vaccination can help prevent most cases of this acute, chronic bacterial infection that affects swine of all ages. Animals have elevated temperatures, are lame, and have poor appetites. If the case becomes chronic, it can affect the heart valves. The bacteria can remain alive in soil, water, pasture, and dead animals. An inflammatory joint disease, erysipelas can exhibit purple diamond- or rhomboid-shaped patches on skin. Antiserum may be administered to animals in contact with carriers.

**Mycoplasmal Polyserositis:** Symptoms are acute lameness with moderate fever, anorexia, and labored breathing. Treatment is possible with antibiotics, but the disease may recur. Treatment is a reduction of stress-causing factors such as cold, hard floors, overcrowding, and large variance in temperature fluctuations.

**Suppurative Arthritis and Osteomyelitis:** This disease can be caused and aggravated by standing or walking on cold, damp surfaces. It occurs mostly in older animals, but it can be found in sucklings. Treat with an antibiotic in the early stages.

**Streptococcal Arthritis:** This disease, found in young pigs 7 to 21 days old, results in swollen joints. Fever or depression may suggest this bacterial disease.

## Reproductive Diseases

**Brucellosis:** This disease is preventable only by purchasing stock from brucellosis-free herds. Brucellosis causes spontaneous abortions, infertility, and sometimes sterility in boars. *Brucella suis*, the disease-causing organism, can be found in contaminated soil. Vaccination is not reliable. Herds should be tested and validated.

**Leptospirosis:** This disease, which causes spontaneous abortions, stillbirths, and baby pigs with low vitality, can be prevented with immunizations every six months, an additional immunization just before breeding, and elimination of stagnant water and poor sanitation. Hosts are cattle, rats, fox, skunks, opossum, and dogs. The spirochete bacterium is shed in urine and mucous-membrane discharges.

**Mastitis, Metritis, Agalactia (MMA):** This syndrome results in death of newborn pigs through starvation and susceptibility to other diseases of the newborn. The sow can be treated with oxytocin, corticosteroids, and antibacterials. Extra support for the babies—fostering them or hand raising, and treating with antibiotics and colostrum replacer—is critical.

**Porcine Parvovirus:** The most common cause of infectious reproductive failure in swine. Infection is by ingestion or contact with an infected environment. It causes fetal death during pregnancy. Sire and dam should be vaccinated as babies and throughout life. The disease infects the lymphatic system and intestinal tract, destroying the delicate lining of the intestines. Shock and death follow unless intensive fluid and antibiotic therapy is administered at once.

**Pseudorabies Virus:** This is a disease of the central nervous system that has symptoms of sneezing and coughing, anorexia, followed by convulsions, coma, and death. Vaccines that are available reduce the risks; however, they do not prevent natural infection. Pigs are the primary hosts and can cause infection of other animals. The disease can also be carried by many mammals and wild birds to your pigs. Infection is by contact with nasal aerosols or by oral ingestion. Control is through periodic blood testing of the herd. Although there is a vaccine available, it interferes with the monitoring of blood testing and is therefore controlled or prohibited by many states. Pigs can also be carriers with no visible signs.

## Other Infectious Diseases

**Porcine Proliferative Enteritis:** This is a common disease of growing or breeding pigs, and causes diarrhea that may have blood in it. Severe cases can cause chronic, irreversible necrotic enteritis. Antibacterial drugs can treat affected animals and those that have been exposed to infected animals.

**Enteric Salmonellosis:** This large- and small-intestine disease is more common in growing and breeding swine. Antibacterial drugs should be given to affected pigs and those in contact with them. Disinfection is essential to prevent epidemic.

**Cholera:** The United States is thought to be cholera-free, and use of vaccines will keep it that way. Symptoms include staggering and purple patches on ears and abdomen. This disease is carried by contaminated stagnant water and poor sanitation.

## Noninfectious Diseases

**Baby Pig Anemia:** A sow's milk is much lower in iron than the amount that is required by baby pigs to make red blood cells; therefore, supplemental iron injection or oral administration of iron to piglets is required immediately after birth. The best methods are

by injection in the ham or neck muscle, or an oral dose of iron dextran.

**Edema D:** This acute, highly fatal disease is a neurological disorder that attacks the small intestine. Abrupt change in diet of weaned pigs may increase the incidence. Gradual dietary change and increase in fiber will help prevent it. Treatment is with antibacterial drugs. Vaccines are ineffective, and predisposition to the disease may be hereditary.

## A Sound Vaccination Program

Your pig can become resistant to certain diseases through immunization. Vaccines are composed of the organisms that cause the particular disease for which resistance is desired. The organisms are killed, or modified so that they can no longer cause that particular disease. The vaccine itself does not protect the animal. Rather, it is the production of antibodies within the animal after immunization that creates the resistance to the disease. If the pig has an immune system that does not respond properly, the vaccine will not result in immunity; vaccines are beneficial only on pigs with normal, balanced immune systems. Many vaccines also must be given at a particular age and sequence. Some are helpful when administered to the pregnant sow, who then produces the antibodies and passes them along to her unborn fetuses and/or via her colostrum. Technology in the field of medicine is rapidly changing. Now synthetic vaccines are being produced, as are some in which the genetic makeup of the organisms is altered.

Before administering any vaccine, check with your veterinarian for the exact dose for your pig. All swine vaccines have directions for large commercial swine that can top the scale at 600 pounds or more. Genetically smaller pigs may receive an antigen overload if the dose for a large pig is given. So little

# Disease Prevention and Control

research has been conducted with small swine that the level of immunity from a reduced dose is not certain at this time.

The following are some of the diseases and organisms for which the pig can be vaccinated:

- *Bordetella bronchiseptica*
- *Clostridium perfringens*
- *E. colibacillosis*
- Erysipelas
- *Haemophilus parasuis*
- *Haemophilus pleuropneumonia*
- Leptospirosis (bratislava, canicola, grippoty phosa, hardjo, icterohaemorrhagiae, pomona)
- Parvovirus
- *Pasteurella multocida*
- Rotavirus
- Swine dysentery (*Treponema hyodysenteriae*)
- Transmissible gastroenteritis

This doesn't meant that your pig must be given fifteen or more vaccinations. Instead, you should plan a sound immunization program for your particular geographical area. Two people can advise you on swine diseases that are prevalent in your area: your veterinarian and your county agent. Your county agent can give you an overview of swine diseases in the county in which you live. Your veterinarian should know of any problems in your immediate area.

Pet pigs require a different and less intensive immunization program than that for breeding pigs. Pigs that attend shows with contestants from outside the county and state will need additional protection. State laws and regulations usually only cover diseases such as leptospirosis, pseudorabies, and brucellosis. Be aware that individual allergic reaction can happen with the introduction of any foreign substance. This can be a general reaction, or a localized reaction, in the form of an abcess, where the vaccine was introduced.

Before selecting an immunization schedule for your pig, consider the following:

- Sex of your pig
- Is it to be a breeder or pet?
- How close are other pigs?
- Prevalence of the diseases in your area?
- Lifestyle of the pig. Will it travel into problem areas, go to shows, etc.?
- What is the safety of the vaccine(s) you are considering?

A suggested immunization schedule for a pet pig (depending on your geographical location) follows:

Three to ten days: Vaccinate for transmissible gastroenteritis
Eight to twelve weeks: Vaccinate for leptospirosis, parvo, erysipelas, haemophilus pleuropneumonia, and tetanus
Twelve to sixteen weeks: Vaccinate for leptospirosis, parvo, erysipelas, Haemophilus pleuropneumonia, tetanus, and rabies (optional)
Semiannual Boosters: leptospirosis, parvo, erysipelas, Haemophilus pleuropneumonia, and tetanus
Annual Boosters: rabies and tetanus

Many vaccines are broad-spectrum combinations and protect against several diseases. If your program includes one of these, your pig will not have to endure quite as many individual injections.

Once you have developed an immunization program with your veterinarian, your pig will receive its first vaccinations. This initial dose is usually repeated in two to six weeks. Depending on the type of vaccine, annual or semiannual boosters are recommended to provide uninterrupted protection. Each vaccine requires a particular method of administration: subcutaneous, intramuscular, or intranasal.

## Appropriate Antibiotic Therapy

Antibiotics and antibacterials are specifically designed to stop or inhibit the invading organism without harm to the animal to which it is administered. Unless you know exactly what specific bacteria or virus you are dealing with, consult your veterinarian. A veterinarian can do a culture and sensitivity test to find the specific microbe that is causing the illness. This test takes from 24 to 72 hours. The test is done from samples taken from one or more of the following: skin scraping, fecal matter, mucus, blood, genital discharge, etc. The matter from these collections is introduced into a sterile medium that is conducive to the growth of bacteria. This medium is treated in certain areas with various antibiotics, and the unit is incubated. The bacteria will be destroyed in all areas to which it is sensitive; therefore the name "culture and sensitivity test." Before the results are reported, the veterinarian may try appropriate antibiotics, relying on his or her experiences with similar situations. Your veterinarian is trained to evaluate these situations in the best interests of your animal.

The easiest way to administer tablets is to hide them in a food treat. A hard plastic or metal animal piller can be used to administer tablets when the pig refuses to eat.

## Giving Medications

Most medication comes in four forms: tablets, powders, liquids, injections.

### Tablets
It is somewhat easy to administer tablets to young pigs. Place them as far back in the mouth as you can, and rub the throat until the pig swallows the tablets. To keep from getting bitten by larger pigs, administer tablets with the help of a balling gun or animal piller. These instruments hold the tablet in one end. When pushed, a plunger expels the tablet. Insert the tablet into the device, place it as far into the mouth as possible, and push the plunger. The tablet is delivered to the back of the throat. If the instrument is plastic, keep it away from the pig's molars so that it is not crushed. Small tablets may also be administered in special treats, such as bananas, apples, and sweet potatoes.

### Liquids
Liquid medications may be added to the feed or water if they are not unpleasant tasting. Add them to a very small amount of food to be sure the pig consumes all the medication. A small dose may be injected into a piece of fruit, such as a grape. Then give the balance of the ration. If the medication is not pleasant tasting, you may have to resort to administering it with a syringe. The size of your pig's mouth and the amount of medication you need

Use your pig's favorite tidbit when teaching it tricks. Here Olivia shows off. Top: The "kneel" is not difficult to teach because it is a natural behavior. Bottom left: The pig can be guided into a sit position with a treat. Bottom right: The "dance" is an extension of the "sit" with the treat just out of reach.

to administer will dictate the size of the syringe. Add an extension tube to the syringe so that you can reach the back of the mouth. This will assure bypassing most of the taste buds and keeping most of the medication in the pig's mouth.

## Powders

Medications in this form should be added to food or treats. If the one you are administering is pleasant tasting, you will not have to try to disguise the taste. If it is bitter, roll it up in a slice of cheese, forming a ball. Give the pig a few pieces of cheese without the medication first, then give it one with the medication.

## Injections

Injections are used for immunizations and administration of medications, electrolytes, vitamins, and minerals. They are usually given by your veterinarian according to the manufacturer's directions. There are several ways to administer injections. The rate of absorption of the medication is dictated by the method of administration. The average pet pig owner may never have to give an injection. If you have no expertise in giving injections, your veterinarian can give you instructions in certain cases. This section is included so you may understand the various methods of injections. Be sure your veterinarian approves of your level of expertise before you practice this type of treatment.

A pig loves to eat more than most anything else. Be sure that treats are wholesome and consist of a food you would normally feed to the pig. It is important that foods used for treats are subtracted from the pig's normal ration so that it does not become obese and unhealthy.

The methods of injections used on pigs in order of absorption rate, fastest first are:
- Intravenous injections, made directly into the bloodstream.
- Intraperitoneal injections, administered into the abdominal cavity on the pig's right side.
- Intramuscular injections, administered into the neck muscles behind the ear or in the thigh muscle.
- Subcutaneous injections, administered between the skin and underlying tissues.
- Intranasal medications, administered into the pig's nostrils, without a needle.

Be absolutely sure to *use the correct method of administration* and to do each injection properly. You should NEVER attempt to perform an injection unless advised to do so by your veterinarian. You might hit a vital nerve, blood vessel, or organ and do more damage than good.

Some injectable medications come in two separate vials. One contains a liquid and the other a powdered or freeze-dried portion. To reconstitute this vaccine, the liquid is first drawn into a syringe and inserted into the dry portion. When it is fully mixed, it is drawn into the syringe and is ready for administration to the patient.

## Parasite Control

Your pig roots in the ground frequently and ingests large amounts of soil and other matter that can contain eggs of various parasites. The parasites will hatch, grow, and migrate to the particular part of the body to which they are adapted. There are various types of parasites: those that live in the ears, on the skin, in the gastrointestinal tract, liver, kidneys, heart, muscles, blood, and other parts of the body.

# Disease Prevention and Control

Sometimes the host pig is directly affected by the parasite itself. In other cases, the important consideration is the damage done by the parasite and the diseases that can invade the damaged tissues. Identification and eradication of the parasites should be of primary concern.

## Internal Parasites (Endoparasites)

Do not routinely deworm without checking a fecal sample. You will not know what type of parasiticide to use unless you identify the parasite. This simple test can help you determine if it is really necessary to deworm your pig, thus saving possibly unnecessary stress to your animal and money for your pocketbook. Collect a fresh fecal sample (a tablespoon is usually more than adequate) and place in a Ziploc bag or empty pill container. Take the sample to your veterinarian.

There is an injectable general wormer that controls many worms and parasites that your pig could be harboring. The weight of the pig must be established to determine the proper dosage. Dewormers should be used alternately with another type of dewormer so that the parasites do not develop a resistance to any one type. There is also a pour-on topical wormer that systemically rids your pig of most internal and external parasites.

When your pig has been treated for parasites and is ready to be reintroduced to its normal surroundings, be certain all fecal matter has been removed. The pig's area and facilities should be thoroughly cleaned before your pig returns. Removal of the pig to another area for several months would greatly help to prevent reinfestation.

Some internal parasites your pig can harbor are:

**Threadworms (*Strongyloides ransomi*):** These burrow into the small intestine and can cause anemia and death.

**Large roundworms (*Ascaris suum*):** Found in the small intestine and migrate to the stomach. They can be 12 inches (30 cm) or more in length and very thick. The eggs are passed in the feces. When they are ingested, they hatch in the intestine, penetrate its wall, and pass into the liver. After growing there, they migrate to the lungs via the bloodstream, eventually returning to the digestive system when the pig swallows its sputum, where they mature. They affect weanlings to adults and can cause severe damage. The migrating larvae can damage liver and lungs and produce conditions favorable for bacterial and viral pneumonias, and diarrhea.

**Whipworms (*Trichuris suis*):** Found in the mucosa of the cecum and colon. In young pigs they can cause bloody diarrhea by accumulating in the cecum and large intestine. Symptoms can be confused with those of dysentery or enteritis.

**Nodular Worms (*Oesophagostomum* sp.):** Found in the large intestine, these worms infect swine of all ages and cause digestive illness and inefficiency.

**Stomach Worms (*Hyostrongylus, Ascarops, and Physochephalus*):** These three types of worms are very common in grazing pigs. Severe gastritis may occur as well as anemia, diarrhea, or weight loss. Swine of all ages can be infested by these worms. which cause inflammation and irritation of the stomach.

**Lungworms (*Metastrongylus*):** Found mostly in older pigs, this parasite migrates to lung tissues, causes bleeding, and allows development of pneumonia. The eggs are passed in the urine. This problem is usually found in subtropical and tropical areas in pigs raised outdoors.

**Kidney Worm (*Stephanurus dentatus*):** Found in older pigs, this parasite damages liver, ureters, and the kidney.

***Isospora suis:*** Can be found in young pigs,

age six days to three weeks. It is a form of coccidiosis. Piglets will be stunted. Thorough cleaning of facilities and fecal removal is imperative.

## External Parasites (Ectoparasites)

External parasites of pigs are easier to diagnose because they are usually visible, or evidenced by the pig's continual scratching. Several treatments are available to eradicate these pests. But since pigs get into and out of water often (and may drink the same water), the water may become contaminated with the insecticides. Be sure you read the insecticide label thoroughly to see if ingestion of the chemical in water is harmful. It might be wise to restrict your pig's access to bathing water until the treatment is complete.

Some external pests your pet might encounter are:

**Hog Louse (*Haematopinus suis*):** This bloodsucking parasite causes irritation, and the pig will vigorously rub its skin against whatever is available. The lice then congregate around the irritated site and cause greater irritation. Pigs with lice do not eat properly and can become depressed. In a single house pet, this condition is rare.

**Hog Mange (*Sarcoptic scabiei suis* and *Demodex suis*):** These are mite-caused contagious skin diseases. There are two types, sarcoptic and demodectic. They cause lesions in the skin because the mites are nourished by the tissues and blood of the pig. Dips, sprays and medicated bedding are recommended to eliminate the mite. Demodectic mange, called "red mange," is caused by a mite that is normally on all pigs. If the pig has a low resistance to this mite, which invades the hair follicles and sweat glands, the mite will take hold and

the symptoms will become manifest. A pig with normal resistance to this mite will rarely have an outbreak.

## Zoonoses

Diseases transmitted between animals and humans are called "zoonoses." Pigs and people can transmit diseases between each other, but the chance of this happening is reduced greatly if the following are practiced:

- Good sanitation
- Rigidly followed vaccination and immunization program
- Regular parasite control
- Proper environment
- Limited or no access to other pigs

Diseases can be transmitted through the skin, inhaled, or ingested. They can be transmitted through direct or indirect contact with bodily fluids, excretions, scratches, wounds, or animal tissue (including an aborted fetus). Mites, mosquitoes, flies, and other intermediate carriers can spread a disease from the infected animal to a human or from a human to an animal.

Common diseases that can be transmitted between swine and people include bacterial disease: anthrax, brucellosis (undulant fever), erysipeloid (erysipelas in swine), leptospirosis, listeriosis, meliodidosis, and salmonellosis; viral diseases: foot and mouth disease, vesicular exanthema, influenza, and parainfluenza; parasitic diseases: Chagas' disease (via the bite of a triatomid bug), sacrosporidiosis, tapeworm (cysticercosis), trichinosis, fleas, mites, and lice; fungal diseases: ringworm.

# First Aid Emergencies

Many techniques used on humans and other animals are applicable to pigs. Consider enrolling in classes for first aid and CPR given by the Red Cross and other organizations. You may wish to read *First Aid for Your Dog*, published by Barron's Educational Series. Remember, your first defense against permanent injury to or death of your pig is your ability to survey the situation and contact your veterinarian without wasting precious time. Often your veterinarian can give you advice over the telephone. The decision to self-treat or have a veterinarian intervene depends on each individual situation: your location, the time of day, type and severity of the injury or trauma, and availability of your veterinarian.

If your pig is injured, remember that it could be very frightened and therefore dangerous. No matter how close your relationship has been, do not take it personally if your pig acts defensively or aggressively toward you or anyone else when it is hurt. Take precautions to protect both yourself and the pig. Wear long sleeves or a jacket, especially if you have a boar with tusks that have not been trimmed or removed. Leather or heavy garden gloves may help prevent injury from bites. But keep in mind that the strength of your grip on the pig may be different than with bare hands, depending on the glove material.

## Call Your Veterinarian Immediately

*The following first-aid procedures are not given as an alternative to veterinary care!* These procedures should be attempted only when there is no veterinarian available, there is no accessible emergency clinic, and you are thoroughly familiar with the procedures. An in-correct or delayed diagnosis can threaten the life of your pig!

## What to Look For

First, check to see if your pig is breathing or is having *difficulty breathing*. This is where it helps to know the normal body rates of your pig. Temperature, respiration, and pulse of your animal can all help you decide what type of first aid it will need. Is it breathing faster? Slower? Irregularly? Is it panting or not breathing at all? Is its temperature more than one degree from its normal either way? Is it in shock or is it stable?

### Attitude

If your pig is *acting aggressively*, cover it with a blanket. Only if absolutely necessary, because of vigorous attempts to bite or slash, muzzle it by looping a strip of cloth around its snout, tying under the chin, bringing the ends behind the ears, and knotting and tying a bow for quick release. Do not muzzle if the pig is having trouble breathing, is panting, or is choking. Muzzling is used only for injuries like bleeding and broken bones, and only when there is a great danger that you could be bitten. When a pig becomes stressed it will become frantic, respiration will be faster, and it may become severely overheated. MAKE EVERY ATTEMPT TO KEEP THE PIG CALM!

### Airway problems

If your pig is having *trouble breathing*, check its mouth and throat for obvious obstructions. If the animal is still choking, it may have swallowed something that must be surgically removed. Remove any blood, vomitus, food, or saliva. Clean the pig's nose. If the pig is not

# First Aid Emergencies

breathing, you may need to apply artificial respiration. The pig's brain can only be without oxygen for about four minutes without sustaining irreversible damage. Lay the pig on its side and try to pull the tongue forward, head and neck forward. Press and release with your hands over its ribs. Repeat approximately 10 times per minute.

If it is necessary to give *mouth-to-nose resuscitation*, clean the nose and mouth, pull the tongue forward, and give about 10 breaths per minute. If the pig starts to breathe on its own, stop. If it tries to vomit or choke, raise its hind legs above the level of its head. Be cautious—you are right in striking range of the pig's teeth and tusks! REMEMBER, A STRESSED PIG CAN BE DANGEROUS!

## Shock

Shock can be caused by many things, including electrocution. This is a real life-threatening emergency. Every attempt should be made to get the pig to a veterinarian. The pig's cardiovascular system is in sudden failure. Brain damage can occur. Indications of shock are fast, weak heartbeat; shallow, fast breathing; pale gums and tongue; low body temperature; unconsciousness; dilated pupils; and staring. (Open the mouth, press on the gums, and watch for a return to normal color. It should take less than two seconds.) On the way to the veterinarian, keep your pig warm, with the head lower than the rest of the body. Keep its mouth clear, and administer artificial respiration or mouth-to-nose respiration. Be aware that the effects of shock can be irreversible and even fatal.

## Bleeding

Bleeding should be treated by applying direct pressure to the wound with a soft gauze pad or compress. Keep pressure applied until bleeding stops. If the cut is superficial, clean the wound with hydrogen peroxide and apply pressure. If it is severe and you can apply a tourniquet, be sure to release it every few minutes to relieve pressure. If your pig is vomiting blood, there may be internal injuries and you will need to get the animal to a vet right away.

## Poisoning

This may be suggested by vomiting, weakness, bleeding, twitching, seizures, salivating, collapse, or staggering. Call your veterinarian, the local poison control center, or the animal center listed in the back of this book. Try to identify the source of the poison. Do not induce vomiting unless instructed to do so. If the ingested substance is caustic, your pig will be injured a second time as it regurgitates the substance. Vomiting should not be induced if the animal is convulsing, unconscious, or depressed. The vomitus could be aspirated into the lungs and cause further problems. If instructed to induce vomiting, use full-strength hydrogen peroxide and a bulb syringe or large plastic syringe. You can also use ipecac syrup at the rate of one teaspoon per five pounds of body weight. Insert this on the side of the mouth, behind the canines and toward the back of the throat.

Take every precaution to avoid accidentally poisoning your pig. Your pig enters life nose first, and continues to use that approach for the remainder of its life. Nearly everything in the pig's life will be tested with its nose and often with its mouth. Remember, a minuscule amount of many substances WILL KILL! So if you are aware of the risks, you will keep potentially toxic substances away from your family, your pigs, and other pets as well. For further information on this subject, write to the National Animal Poison Information Network Association. The address and phone number are available in the Sources section of this book.

A toxic substance can gain entry into your animal's body in several ways, not just through ingestion. Poisons can enter your pig's system by direct contact with the skin, eyes, or ears, or through inhalation. The body has many defense mechanisms that try to detoxify a system that has been invaded by a poisonous substance. Even if the body is detoxified, major damage can happen to the organs (liver, kidneys, lung, digestive tract, etc.) that helped detoxify it.

If you suspect poisoning, collect samples of urine, vomit, and feces in clean containers like Ziploc bags. Get your animal to a veterinary emergency center immediately. If you know what your pig has ingested, inhaled, etc., take that container with you if possible. Otherwise, take down what information you can from the label.

Do not induce vomiting or give any fluids unless you have been advised to do so by a competent professional. You may interfere with subsequent treatment, such as induced vomiting, purging the stomach by washing, adding absorbents to bind toxins, dilution, antidotes, etc. Keep the animal warm until you get to the veterinarian.

To treat your animal, you must prevent further exposure to and absorption of the toxic substance. Use appropriate antidotes, and provide therapy for the animal's condition, which may include support of the cardiovascular, respiratory, and nervous systems.

Many chemicals, plants, and food items that are found in and around our homes are potentially harmful to your pig. Use good sense and make sure that your pig's environment is "pig-proof." There are many chemicals used today as additives in all types of products that are potentially dangerous to you or your animals. Out of sight is not out of mind! Pigs can

learn to open cabinet doors. READ THE LABEL on everything for the benefit of you, your family, and your animals. The following section lists many toxic substances, but does not cover each and every possibility.

Some symptoms of poisoning are: convulsions, labored breathing, seizures, salivation, vomiting, muscle spasms, elevated temperature, weakness, uncoordination, nasal secretion, diarrhea, dehydration, disorientation, staggering, stumbling, and loss of sight or hearing. Remember, know your pig and its normal behavior. Be aware of any unusual change, and take action if necessary.

Everything we eat is *not* good for animals, and some of it is not good for us either!

## Types of Poisoning

**Acorn Poisoning:** Your pig can develop laminitis (hoof inflammation) from eating too many acorns. Take this into consideration when planning a recreation site for it under an oak tree.

**Algal Poisoning:** It is important to keep the pig's drinking water free of toxic blue-green algae. High concentrations can cause poisoning. Water placed in direct sunlight will have a higher incidence of this type of algae. This type of poisoning is totally preventable by using proper sanitation measures.

**Antifreeze (Ethylene Glycol):** This is a frequent seasonal problem. It may be in runoff on the ground from a car. Its sweet taste is palatable. Death is common.

**Arsenic Poisoning:** Products containing arsenic have seen diminishing usage, so there is now little incidence of this type of poisoning today. There are some arsenic products used today for animal and poultry dips, and some used to actually improve production in swine and poultry. If an animal ingests too much of this chemical, poisoning will occur.

# First Aid Emergencies

**Bracken Fern Poisoning:** Bracken fern is distributed over most of North America. As the plant is consumed, it accumulates in the animal, until a level of toxicity is reached that will produce symptoms. Besides being toxic, it is a carcinogen after long-term, low levels of consumption.

**Blister Beetle:** Check all alfalfa hay for blister beetle contamination. Just one dead beetle can kill an animal. There is no treatment for this poisoning. The three species of blister beetles range over most of the United States and Canada. Strangely, the larvae of two species (*Epicanta vittata* and *Lytta magister*) of the blister beetle are beneficial to agriculture because they parasitize grasshopper eggs. The adult beetles, however, can be serious defoliating crop pests. The insect is 3/8 to to 1/8 inches (9–28 mm) long, with a soft body, broad head, and long narrow body. One species is striped black and tan. If you see any insects, dead or alive, in hay you purchase, take a sample to your county agent for identification.

**Chemicals:** Many chemicals that are useful in agriculture and also home use are highly toxic to animals if ingested. These chemicals are many and include: insecticides, herbicides, fertilizers, cleaning products, soap, detergent, alkali batteries, ammonia, disinfectants, antiseptics, boric acids, alcohol, bleach, antirust compounds, antifreeze, motor oil, paints, thinners, kerosene, heating oils, furniture polish, paint removers and thinners, windshield washer fluid, snail baits, ant poisons, gasoline, wood treatments (creosote), and mercury.

**Chocolate and Caffeine (Methylxanthine):** These are found in chocolate, cocoa products, colas, and some over-the-counter drugs. If your pig ingests these it may exhibit vomiting, restlessness, hyperactivity, excessive urination, and/or elevated heart and respiratory rates. Although deaths are rare, heart irregularities, weakness, and seizures may occur. Baking chocolate is especially dangerous, since it is eight times more potent than regular chocolate.

**Drugs, Legal and Illegal:** Allergy medications, sleep aids, vitamins, topical products, inflammatory drugs, cold and cough medicines, laxatives, antacids, aspirin, and many more. Caffeine, amphetamines, cocaine, hallucinogens, barbiturates, and opiates can cause serious damage or death to your pig.

**Illicit Drugs and Plants:** Marijuana, jimsonweed, thorn apple, trumpet vine, peyote, mescal, morning glory, nutmeg, periwinkle, and certain wild mushrooms.

**Lead Poisoning:** This can be caused by ingesting lead-based paints, batteries, linoleum, water pipes, dies, shotgun pellets, putty, certain greases, caulking, fishing weights, inks, and dyes. Lead-based paints have a sweet taste that is appealing to the pig. Treatment is possible, and effective. Lead-based paints were banned in the United States in 1970, but many buildings that were painted with lead-based paint before then flake and peel, and these chips of paint can easily be ingested by a pig. Brain damage can occur from just a few flakes of ingested paint, especially if eaten by a very young pig. To be sure your pig is safe, flaking paint can be tested to see if it contains lead. Even paint that does not contain lead can be toxic, so be aware of any painted surface your pig can chew or lick.

**Molds and Fungi:** Toxic molds or fungi are found on peanuts, soybeans, cottonseed mean, rice, sorghum, corn, seed heads of grasses, barley, pastures, seed pods, rye, grain meal, clover, moldy feed, etc. Be alert and check pastures periodically for mushrooms or diseased plants. Also, watch to see that foodstuffs do not get wet, or contain molds or fungi.

**Rodent Poisons:** Watch for anticoagulant

rat or mouse poisons, which will cause hemorrhaging in your pig. Your pig can hemorrhage from the nose, mouth, rectum, and bladder. Some rat poisons work on the nervous system, causing seizures, depression, lack of coordination, and death. Cholecalciferol (vitamin D analog) rat poisons disrupt the normal calcium balance, causing excessive calcium in the blood. Treatment includes removing the excessive calcium.

**Selenium:** This mineral is found naturally in many soils that pigs in contact with the soil ingest naturally as a matter of rooting behavior. If your pig is never on soil, or your soil is selenium-deficient, feed a vitamin supplement with added selenium. Too much can be toxic!

**Sodium Chloride (Salt) Poisoning:** High levels of salt in the body of a pig caused by excessive ingestion of salt and inadequate (or excessive) ingestion of water can cause serious and rapid health changes, including death.

**Zinc Poisoning:** If your pig ingests pennies, zinc oxide skin ointment, galvanized metals, nails, fertilizers, some medications, sun-blocking lotions, shampoos, etc., it may intoxicate itself with excessive zinc. Treatment is possible.

## Toxic Plants and Plant Parts

The list of plants and plant parts that are toxic is seemingly endless, but I will list all we know at this time. If you want your pig around a long time, be aware that everything is potential food to it. Be sure it is not toxic, if you are not sure, remove it. Be careful of spraying or treating anything in your pig's surroundings that it might come in bodily contact with including its grazing area. If you have a house pig, you will become aware in short order that everything in your backyard is a potential meal for your pig. Fruit trees, roses, and any plants, that have leaves fragrant to the pig will be pruned relentlessly. The pig's sensitive nose will search out your flower bulbs, many of which are toxic to animals. Although in most instances pigs will not eat plants that are dangerous, do not take the chance by having any around the area your pig can reach. Remember, just a leaf or two of certain plants (oleanders, for one) mixed in with other foods or grasses can kill your pet.

Some plants in the following lists have only parts that are poisonous like new shoots, bark, bulbs, seeds, needles, leaves, or pods. Others are poisonous only in large amounts, or when the second growth has occurred due to drought or heavy fertilization.

**Spring:** Bitterweed, pingue, sacaahuista, beargrass, water hemlock, larkspur, pokeweed, cocklebur, African rue, greasewood, false hellebore, horsebrush, death camas, buckeye, fly poison, staggergrass, crow poison, lantana, oaks (buds and acorns).

**Summer:** Mesquite, yellow star thistle, yellow knapweed, red maple, perilla mint, beefsteak plant, prickly copperweed, white snakeroot, nightshades, Jerusalem cherry, potato, horsenettle, buffalo bur, dogbanes.

**Fall or Winter:** Rayless, goldenrod, burroweed, halogeton, mescal bean, frijolito, mountain laurel, jimmy fern, cloak fern, bladderpod, rattlebox, sesbane, coffee bean, china berry.

**All Year:** Silverling, baccharis, yerba de pasmo, bracken fern, chokecherry, wild cherry, peach, guajillo, lechequilla, milkweed, locoweed, milkvetch, *astragalus*, inkweed,

Miniature pigs love to graze on grass and plants. Check to see that no toxic plants are in the area and that no harmful chemicals or fertilizers have been used on any plant material it may consume. Rooting behavior is a part of grazing and is performed when the pig is looking for succulent roots or grubs—or just for the love of rooting.

drymary, broomweed, snakeweed, slinkweed, turpentine weed, paper flowers, groundsel, *senecio*, arrowgrass, Saint. John's wort, goatweed, Klamath weed, corn cockle, orange sneezeweed, smallhead, lupines, bluebonnet, poison hemlock, *crotalaria*, rattlebox, jimsonweed, thorn apple, yellow jesamine, evening trumpet, Carolina jessamine, laurel, ivy bush, lambkill, oleander, laurel cherry, castor bean, sorghum, Sudan, kafir, durra, milo, broomcorn, schrock, Johnson grass, western yellow pine, mustard, crucifers, cress.

## Heatstroke

This may be indicated by panting, collapse, unconsciousness, drooling saliva, and/or rattling respiration. Put a cold compress on the pig's head, and use a garden hose with cold water to bring its temperature down. Cold enemas can also be given. Be sure to continually check the pig's temperature so that it does not get too low; failure to do so may result in hypothermia.

## Broken Bones, Fractures, Dislocations

Transporting your pig to your veterinarian with these types of injuries should be attempted with great care and caution. Use the proper restraint and a muzzle, if necessary, since the animal will be in great pain. Control any bleeding as suggested above. Strap the pig to a board by placing a towel or blanket over the body portion and then tying at least three straps around the body and the board. This

Baby pigs are cute and irresistible. Whenever possible, try to see the parents of the piglet you wish to purchase so you will have an idea of the pig's eventual adult size.

should adequately restrain the pig and prevent further injury until you reach your veterinarian. If you are certain the break is in a longbone, a temporary splint should be applied before transporting the pig.

## Electrical Shock

Your pig likes to chew things and is very oral about his world. He could bite through an electrical cord in a heating pad or extension cord. Be sure there are no cords within reach of your pig that are not properly covered with some type of conduit. A simple wire covering can be made by slipping a piece of PVC pipe over the wire and securing both ends with tape. If you see your animal bite an electrical cord and it is being shocked, unplug the cord at its source. Do not touch the animal until the cord is unplugged. If you cannot find the plug, shut off the breaker or if necessary, the main switch. While standing on dry ground, push the animal away with a dry wooden pole. Establish breathing and heartbeat (CPR) and treat for shock and burns. Keep the animal quiet and warm, clear its air passages, and take it to the veterinarian. Fluids can be given carefully by mouth if you cannot obtain professional care immediately. A saline solution can be used: two tablespoons salt and one tablespoon of baking soda to three pints of water given at the rate of 10 percent of the weight of the animal per day for the first day and 5 percent the second day.

## Wounds

The tetanus spore (*Clostrodium tetani*) is soil-borne and introduced through wounds, especially deep puncture wounds. Incubation is 10 to 14 days or more.

If your pig gets a deep puncture wound, consult your veterinarian about tetanus antitoxin. This will give immediate protection.

Tetanus toxoid is an annual vaccination used as a preventative, but it will not afford immediate immunity.

## Prevention

- Be certain your pig never gets overheated and has plenty of shade and fresh water.
- Keep electrical cords and appliances out of your pig's reach.
- Be sure there are not sharp or dangerous objects in the animal's area.
- Do not keep two pigs together that have a potential for fighting.
- Be sure your pig's area is secure and that it cannot get out.
- Be sure other animals, especially dogs, cannot get into your pig's area.
- Do not let your pig have toys it can swallow, and be sure there are no small objects in the pig's area.
- Keep nails, razor blades, nail files, sewing needles, pins, etc.,out of your pig's reach.
- Your pig will mouth and taste many things, so keep all toxic substances out of its area. For example, do not spray its grazing area with chemicals that have a residual effect. Be careful if your pig roams over an area where a car may have leaked antifreeze.

## Handling Stress

Any person who owns or works with a pig should be aware that pigs can be stressed very easily. The bloodcurdling screams you hear when pigs are restrained, vaccinated, or treated might make you think that they are overdramatic. Although they really are very dramatic, the *stress* causes the harm to the pig, not what we are doing to it. I cannot overemphasize the need for careful monitoring of any pig that is screaming and being stressed; the animal could easily become a medical problem.

Remember, we are not hurting the pig, the stress is. It can kill a pig. Still, some strains of pigs are more susceptible to porcine stress syndrome than are others. If you suspect that your pig has a genetic weakness in this area, a blood sample can be taken and tested for CPK (creatine phosphokinas, a serum enzyme). Pigs with this tendency have less than perfect circulation and develop metabolic acidosis during stress.

Gentle, proper training methods will nearly eliminate the chance of stressing your pig. But be aware that whenever you must force a pig to have something done to it that it doesn't like, even the gentlest of pigs can become stressed beyond safe levels. Though we do not want to teach the pig that screaming will bring it relief, we must release the pig in a safe area until it has calmed down.

## Treatment of the Convalescent

Getting your pig over the illness or emergency is just the first step in returning it to a healthy state. At this point, the pig is in a weakened condition, and any number of things could go wrong in its body because of the recent trauma. Keep the pig comfortable and free of stress. Monitor temperature, respiration, pulse, and urinary output. Check the color of the mucous membranes. Strictly follow the vet's instructions, including those on feeding and administering of medications.

# Anatomy and Physiology

A general understanding of the various parts of a pig's body and how they work will help you when you visit your veterinarian or have conversations with other pig enthusiasts. With pigs, beauty is indeed more than skin deep! The intelligent pig makes up for its unique outward appearance with great strength and an ability to adapt to many different and varied environments. Pigs are monogastric, which means they have a simple stomach much like our own. They live to eat! They are omnivorous, which means they eat both plant and animal matter. In fact, they sample just about anything that remotely resembles food. In the wild, therefore, they are not highly specialized and have spread over most land areas in varying habitats, from swamps to forests, to plains, in both hot and cold climates. Their adaptability to various terrains, climates, and foods have made them a very widespread and successful animal in the evolutionary tree.

Pigs have a keen sense of smell, and use their snout to locate and "root out" food. While doing so, they consume varying amounts of soil that contains trace minerals. Wild pigs eat roots, plants, insects, small animals, eggs, snakes, and just about anything that won't eat them first. Farmers have long worried about the foolish chicken that gets into the pigpen by mistake. In the wild, pigs are creatures of habit and maintain regular paths, wallows, salt licks, and resting places for a lifetime. As long as the food in an area holds out, the pig family will maintain that area as their home. This nonspecialized preference for food types is precisely what has made the pig family a strong survivor.

We must remember that while pigs are not human, their gregarious behavior makes them perfect candidates to live within human boundaries and to bond to humans.

## Dentition

The formula for a pig's permanent dentition is 3/3, 1/1, 4/4, 3/3. This means there are three incisors, one canine, four premolars and three molars on each side of both the top and bottom, for a total of 44 teeth. The formula for deciduous teeth is 3/3, 1/1, 3/3. This means that there are three incisors, one canine, and three premolars on each side of both the top and bottom, for a total of 28 teeth.

The eruption of the pig's teeth is as follows:

|  | Deciduous | Permanent |
| --- | --- | --- |
| Incisor 1 | 2–4 weeks | 12 months |
| Incisor 2 | 6–12 weeks | 16–20 months |
| Incisor 3 | Before birth | 8–12 months |
| Canine | Before birth | 6–10 months |
| Premolar 1 | None | 5 months |
| Premolar 2 | 5–7 weeks | 12–15 months |
| Premolar 3 | 1–4 weeks | 12–15 months |
| Premolar 4 | 1–4 weeks | 12–15 months |
| Molar 1 | None | 4–6 months |
| Molar 2 | None | 8–12 months |
| Molar 3 | None | 18–20 months |

The canines, called tusks especially on boars, are hollow and grow upward continuously. On boars they can become very long. The tusks wear against each other, sharpening themselves simultaneously. These tusks can become as sharp as a knife blade, and extremely dangerous. As the animal gets older, many teeth loose their enamel and disappear altogether.

## Snout and Smell

Although we think of a pig's snout as hairless, it has many short hairs scattered over its surface. The snout contains the nostrils and many glands. It is movable by the pig at will, and contains a cartilaginous disc. This disc is further supported and strengthened by an unusual bone, the prenasal, below the tip of the skull's nasal bones. Though it is used as a tool by the pig, for digging and rooting, it is a very sensitive part of its body. Farmers take advantage of this sensitivity by placing one or more rings through its top portion to prevent commercial pigs from engaging in undesirable rooting.

The pig has a very keen sense of smell; they can locate minuscule amounts of food in the soil, and follow it by air-scenting. Pigs can be more selective about what they eat than people think. They also will take unusual substances into their mouth to "taste" and smell. Farmers in France capitalize on this keen talent by using pigs to locate highly prized truffles underground. Boars use the combination of smell and taste to sense when a sow is receptive. Pigs are now being widely used by law-enforcement agencies in Germany to "sniff out" drugs, much as drug-sniffing dogs have been used for years. The idea has caught on in the midwestern United States, where Vietnamese pigs are now being trained as "drug-sniffers."

## Eyes and Vision

The eyes of pigs are small and are positioned for good lateral vision. Although their ancestors were nocturnal, pigs do not possess the inner-eye reflective tissue, or "tapetum lucidum," that is thought to contribute to night vision. Nor do they have the well-developed eye muscles needed for sharp focusing, and therefore they are not thought to have very good eyesight. Many authorities believe that the pig is nearsighted.

## Ears and Hearing

All wild swine have upright ears, and domestic swine have ears ranging from upright to lopped. All swine have very good hearing, and when they are alarmed and trying to distinguish a sound, they will freeze and hold their breath while trying to figure out what the sound is and where it is coming from.

## Nervous System

The pig's nervous system is very similar to our own. The structure of the pig's nervous system is inherited from the parents by the offspring, just as is coat color, ear shape, etc. The temperament of an animal is directly related to its physiologically inherited nervous system and further modified by learned behaviors and environment. Therefore, breeders pick parents with gentle natures, good mothering instincts, and low suspicion levels.

## Skin

The thick, firm skin has a few sweat glands and is covered to varying degrees with bristles. During very hot weather and usually twice each year, a large portion of these bristles is shed. On some males, a heavy armor plate of

# Anatomy and Physiology

skin will develop from the shoulders back to the hip. Pigs are very susceptible to sunburn, even the darker-colored pigs. Wild pigs and domestic pigs alike will seek shade during the sunny time of a warm day. Some sunbathing is done on very cold, bright days.

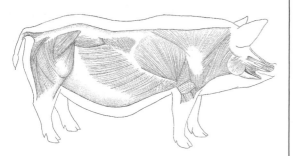

The superficial muscles of the pig.

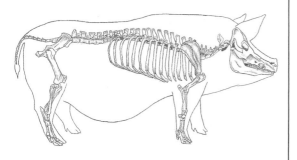

The skeleton of the pig.

## Muscles

The pig is very heavily muscled for its size. The domestic breeds show a greater degree of muscling, due to genetic selection by man.

## Skeletal System

The skeletal system of a pig is very strong and supports great weights in proportion to its size. Think about the amount of surface area a pig's foot covers and the amount of weight that is supported in comparison to our own. The feet on a 100-pound pig support about 8 pounds per square inch. Consider that the feet of a 150-pound person with size eight shoes support about 1.8 pounds per square inch. The average number of ribs is around 14 pair, but bacon-type pigs have up to 17 pair.

## Legs and Feet

The pig's legs are short in comparison to the body. The forelegs are generally one-half the height at the shoulders. Some domestic breeds and wild species have longer legs. The foot contains four hoofed toes. The first digit is missing. The middle two, the third and fourth digits, are larger and touch the ground, while the second and fifth digits (called dewclaws) are raised behind the other two. The dewclaws touch the ground only when the foot sinks into softer ground or the animal is traveling at great speed. Each toe is similar to a finger with a nail wrapped around it. The bottom of each hoof has a soft, fleshy, finger-like portion that becomes callused with age and use.

# *Anatomy and Physiology*

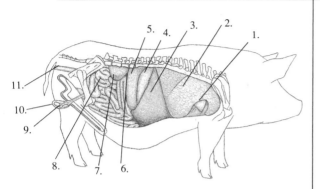

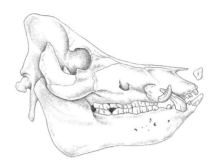

The skull of an adult boar. Note the overlapping tusks.

**The internal organs of the pig.**

1. Heart  2. Lung  3. Liver  4. Stomach  5. Spleen  6. Colon  7. Kidney  8. Small intestine  9. Bladder  10. Testis  11. Rectum

## Locomotion

When pigs are covering ground, trotting and occasional pacing is their normal gait, although they can gallop for short distances. Pigs are not good jumpers, probably due to their short legs, but don't make a big bet your pet pig will not be able to make it up on the bed or your favorite chair if it really wants to.

Pigs are good swimmers. Pigs with potbellies, however, have a tendency to injure their stomachs with their hind hooves while swimming.

Pigs usually begin their daily activities at dawn. They do most of their moving during the day. Dusk usually finds them returning to their nest or den.

## Respiratory System

The pig's respiratory system is similar to our own, but since pigs' snouts are constantly in soil they are more susceptible to invading viruses and bacteria. Respiratory illnesses can be of great concern to pig owners. Breeding for too short of a snout will increase the incidence of breathing and respiratory problems.

## Digestive System

Pigs are monogastric, which means they have a simple stomach system much like our own. Their food needs some chewing before swallowing to aid in digestion. In the dog, by comparison, little chewing is done before swallowing. These animals live to eat; indeed, their whole lives revolve around eating and reproduction. Because pigs are omnivorous, they can digest a variety of foodstuffs. It takes 24 hours for a pig's stomach to completely empty.

## Urinary System

The kidneys of swine are smooth, much like ours, and are not lobulated, as in cattle. Because they perform in the same manner as human kidneys, the pig is used extensively in kidney research.

# Understanding Miniature Pigs

Pigs have several unique behaviors and natural tendencies. These include rooting, wallowing, scratching, playing, and defining toilet areas.

If you understand these behaviors and realize that they are natural, normal, and instinctual for most pigs, you will save yourself much grief raising a pet pig. Understanding them will help you satisfy your pig's natural urges and even use these behaviors to your advantage while raising and training your pigs.

All of these behaviors and tendencies are as natural for a pig as it is natural for you to scratch an irritating itch or look for a glass of water when you are thirsty. In certain cases, you can help the pig redirect these instincts in a way that is agreeable to you and your environment.

## Rooting

Rooting behavior is a manifestation of the pig's natural desire to search out and sample things in its environment with its highly specialized snout. It will unearth roots, grubs, and worms in any available soil, especially if it is confined to a small area or if it becomes bored. It will make no distinction between a pasture, a lawn, and your bed of prize roses. It will plow up any available dirt in its pen searching for something—anything! If the pig is confined in a pen, give it some hay to root in and chew up. It will spend countless hours sorting through the hay and rearranging it. If the pig is uncomfortably warm, it will try to find a resting place for itself in the damp earth by rooting a cool spot in the earth.

If the pig is a house pet, it could root up the carpet in your living room. To stop this undesirable behavior, you must give the pig a substitute outlet, instead of punishing it *after* it does something wrong. Give it some old

blankets and towels that it can root under, and realize that you must live with little piles of blankets here and there on your floor if you wish to have a pig that is satisfied and well adjusted. Otherwise, the pig can turn your wall-to-wall carpet into an assortment of scatter rugs in short order.

## Wallowing

Wallowing behavior is an all-time favorite pastime of swine. Although they prefer fresh mud, they will settle for fresh earth they have just rooted up or hay they have chewed up into small pieces and arranged and rearranged. House pigs will settle for a pile of blankets and towels. A hot-weather treat for outdoor pigs is a child's small wading pool. Pigs will make a wallow out of hay and dirt. Even pigs with well-lubricated skin seem soothed by the action of wallowing. A pig will try to get into any water that is available. It will make no distinction between a 5-gallon bucket of water and a cup full of water. It will try to push both over with its nose and then wallow in the mess it has made.

## Scratching

Scratching (and rubbing) and pigs just go together. Practice proper skin care by keeping the pig free of mites, lice, mange, and dry skin. Use of appropriate insecticides and lubricating oils will reduce scratching to a minimum. Even a "well oiled" pig cannot resist a tummy scratch. You can teach your pig to "play dead" by scratching its side. It will fall over to expose more scratching area as if it has just lapsed into a coma. It will remain there enjoying the massage, lifting each leg as you approach the area underneath it, with its eyes looking at you adoringly. Your fingers will give up long before your pig will tire of the attention. See the sections on external parasites and skin care to help your pig live a comfortable life.

## Playing

Playing is part of most pigs' daily routine. Pigs like to play. They love to chase each other and play with "toys." You don't need to spend *any* money at the toy store. Instead, you can recycle unwanted household items that can become toys for a pig, like an old plastic bucket or milk jug, a cardboard box, burlap sacks, strips of cloth tied to the fence, and whatever else you have that will not be harmful to your pig. Pigs love to tug on them, root them around, and chew on them. Don't use containers that have held any toxic ingredients, including antifreeze. See "Poisoning," page 51 for a list of dangerous substances. Remember, if a toy gets soiled by feces, be sure to remove it and wash it, or it will be ignored and forgotten forever.

## Defined Toilet Areas

Pigs are *naturally neat!* They will use defined toilet areas. A portion of each pig's environment will be designated by the pig itself as the place it relieves itself. Even if you keep several pigs in one contained area, they will normally use the same one or two areas for urinating and defecating. This will later be discussed under "Housebreaking," page 70.

## Cleanliness

Pigs are exceptionally neat when given the opportunity to be so. The old expression about being "dirty as a pigpen" is completely unfounded. Pigs only become dirty when kept in surroundings that *prevent them from being clean*.

If you keep water out of reach (except drinking water), and remove excrement daily, you will find that a pig is as clean as, if not cleaner than, any dog or cat you have ever known.

As mentioned above, pigs have very defined toilet areas, even those pigs that live in the wild. Most of the domestic pig's wild cousins, such as warthogs and European boars, will also defecate and urinate in defined areas. Other pigs in their herd will use the same areas. Pigs *never* soil their den or nesting place.

Dogs tend to relieve themselves anywhere

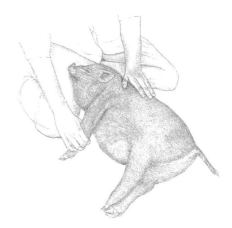

Kindness and consistency in training and discipline will be rewarded with a very special bond between pig and owner. Gentle scratching and massaging of the pig will deepen the human-animal bond.

they see fit at the time, if they have a large area from which to choose. House pigs, when trained to relieve themselves outside, will usually pick one tiny area as their bathroom. For you, cleanup is a breeze. Because pigs also graze on the grass in the yard, they choose to "do their business" in an area that will not interfere with their grazing. This "defined toilet area" helps make pigs very easy to housetrain. They can be trained to use a litter box or go to the door and let you know when they want to go out. With respect to the latter, they can be trained to use a free-swinging doggie door, or to push a button that opens a door to the outside.

If you regularly bathe your pig and condition its skin, it will not shed like most cats and dogs. If given blankets to wallow and root in, they are less apt to co-opt other items in your home as their own.

## Bodily Contact

Pigs have much bodily contact with other pigs of their group during rest and play. They are fond of massaging each other with their snouts. Mothers push their babies about while foraging, as if they are teaching them how to find food. Boars can be very aggressive to each other, pushing or biting. Their large canines, called tusks, can do serious damage if the fight is in earnest. Piglets often argue over the best teats, but they will usually establish territory and select their own nipple(s). Many types of animals, such as horses and cattle, keep their herd together by maintaining visual contact. Pigs, however, with their poorer eyesight, use bodily contact and various auditory signals to maintain their bonds.

## Language

Pigs have a language all their own. They are very vocal, and communicate by grunting, squealing, and snorting to indicate pleasure, distress, alarm, mating, challenge, or for calling their young. It is not difficult for a human to distinguish the pig's various types of communication. The sounds of many animals are universal and distinguishable by other species. Pigs, too, respond to similar sounds from humans. Unlike birds that sing to each other or mimic human voices, pigs maintain their own language. They will try to communicate with you, all the while assuming that you understand them completely. You will know you have reached your pig's heart, and have become a herd member, when it greets you with a "conversation" about how the day has been and how glad it is to see you. That it is really talking to you and verbalizing its pleasure about your presence is unmistakable.

## Social Dominance

Pigs are one of the few animals that establish social dominance at a very early age. Piglets establish "teat territory" within a day or two of birth: One piglet jealously defends the teat it has chosen by biting and chasing off invaders. This territorial behavior is carried through the rest of their lives, during feeding and courtship. Because domestic pigs rarely have to search out their food sources, much of this behavior is not evident. But, when several pigs are fed together in the same trough or container, the behavior is unmistakable.

# *Understanding Miniature Pigs*

## Sideswiping

Sideswiping is a behavior exhibited by a pig that is agitated or irritated. The pig will make a sideways motion with its head toward the pig with which it is angry. Wild relatives of the domestic pig have long tusks that they use for fighting and slashing their opponents. The sideswiping motion is probably a modified version of this wild behavior.

Pet pigs will occasionally exhibit sideswiping at their owners. They do not have tusks (unless they are boars), and contact is rarely made. It is important to know that when your pig exhibits this behavior, it is very agitated.

## Communicating with Your Pig

Pigs communicate with each other through a series of grunts, squeals, and other noises. If you put two strange pigs on opposites sides of a fence, you will hear the interaction between them. Pigs can learn to respond to our voices. When training your pig, use its name and a verbal command combined with a hand signal. Although a pig does not have good eyesight, it can see your hand signal and will soon learn to respond to it as well as to your verbal commands. Let the pig know, with verbal reinforcement, when you are pleased or displeased with its behavior.

## Your Pig's Mind

*A pig can, because it thinks it can.*

There is really only one effective method to train a pig. That is by positive reinforcement. When the pig does something you want it to do, you reward it by giving it something it wants or doing something to it that it likes.

With a pig, positive reinforcement usually means food. A pig will do more for a tidbit than it will for a "thank you." It is not necessary to give the pig a large treat every time you need to reinforce a behavior. The pig will work just as well for a raisin as it will for half of an apple. The pig should be moderately hungry, but not starving, when it is in a training session. If it is very hungry, it may bite your fingers in the excitement, or be so interested in the treats that it cannot concentrate on what it must do to get them. Keep the number of treats moderate, so that your training session ends with the pig still slightly hungry. When a pig is in a structured training program, a large part of its daily ration can be fed during the training sessions, with the balance given later in the day as a meal.

It is almost impossible to train a pig by force. You will notice that even the most gentle pig will resist being forced. If you think of how a wild pig's life differs in nature from that of the dog or cat family, it may help you realize why they are so resistant. In the wild, the dog and cat family are predators. They are not hunted, but do the hunting. Pigs, however, are the hunted; the unlucky pig that does not resist being forced down strongly enough becomes the meal of the one doing the forcing.

Most tricks that are performed by pigs are modified *natural behaviors*. It is difficult to train a pig to do a trick that is not a natural behavior. The pig's anatomy, combined with its mental capabilities, set the perimeters for its learning abilities. For example, pigs cannot do the "roll over" trick that most dogs learn in short order. Pigs do not roll over, as a rule, in everyday situations; therefore, it is impossible to teach that maneuver to them. Forcing a pig into that position is not possible without earsplitting screams and a fight for its life. Even a pig that is well acquainted with you will rarely relax when forced. A pig that does

# Understanding Miniature Pigs

not know you and has not been properly socialized and gentled will go on resisting and screaming until you release it. Understanding this part of a pig's natural instincts is *critical* if you are to be successful in training it. When you do grooming and massaging behavior *to a pig that trusts you*, amazing things happen. It will stretch and fall over on its side, exposing its most vulnerable belly area for additional attention. Using this natural tendency, you will be able to teach your pig to "roll over and play dead" by scratching its side and belly. To get the behavior you want, you must modify things that pigs do naturally.

Another natural behavior you can capitalize on in training is the pig's tendency to use their highly specialized snout for many things. There are many tricks that can be taught by reinforcing this behavior at the proper time.

You must be patient, kind, and fair. Do not lose sight of your goals and the reasons for training your pig. You are doing it for fun, but to keep a willing student, it must be fun for the pig also. Happy pigs learn faster, learn more, and retain the lessons longer than unhappy pigs. If you expect an instant response and are an impatient person, do not try to train your pig. Your frustration will be picked up by your pig and you will end up with an untrained, unhappy pig.

Watch your pig in everyday situations and see what its actions can tell you. Does it take its towel or blanket in its mouth when it goes to bed and pull it over itself? Reinforce this behavior by telling it "Go to bed" when it begins the behavior on its own. Give a small food reinforcement when it completes the action, and you will have a trick pig who is a "pig in a blanket." Your ingenuity and creativeness can develop your pig's individual talents and make it a real show pig. Your friends and neighbors will be impressed when you tell your pig, "It's time for bed," and it gets into its bed and pulls the blanket over itself.

Watch and observe your pig as you introduce it to new situations, pets, and objects. Be ready with treats to reinforce any desirable behavior.

When you fully understand what it means to enhance and modify a pig's natural tendencies, begin with as young a pig as you can. The younger it is, the more receptive its mind will be to new learning experiences, and it will have no bad habits.

Never train more than one pig at a time. They will not only fight over the food, they will forget the action for which they are being reinforced. The one *not* getting the treat will become aggressive and nippy. This undesirable behavior will then have to be corrected. Remember, it is easier to prevent unwanted behavior than to correct it.

# *Training Your Pig*

## The Key Words in Training

The secret of training your pig can be summarized in three words: patience, reward, and discipline.

One of the goals when training your pig is to begin and end with a happy student. A happy pig can learn, an unhappy or frightened pig cannot. To achieve a joyful attitude in your pig student, you should understand how you can motivate your pig and what type of discipline, if any, you can use.

In any training session, you must first get the pig's attention and then hold it. At the same time, you will be trying to prompt it to perform a particular act. When the act is performed, the pig must be rewarded. Two criteria are critical:

1. Timing of the reward
2. Giving a reward the pig considers worth the effort

## Reward

The reward must be given to the pig at a precise time so that it understands that receiving the reward is a consequence of performing the act. If the reward is given too soon, the pig will concentrate on the reward instead of the act it is performing. If the reward is given too late, the pig will not associate its bestowal with the act.

The reward that is most effective in persuading a pig to master a particular act is, of course, food! Choose a healthy food that is irresistible to the pig and easy for you to carry in your pocket. Good choices are raisins, grapes, alfalfa pellets, and Cheerios. Do not use candy or anything containing chocolate. Teach your pig to take food from your hand gently and without snapping. Do not hold the food out of reach so that your pig becomes frantic and snaps to get it. Put the food on the palm of your hand so that no fingers are in the way. The pig must learn that the food you offer is only for it. Never offer treats to more than one pig or pet at the same time. Competition will cause a frenzy, with your fingers in the middle, and the pig will get the blame. When your pig takes treats too roughly, a light bump on the nose, at the moment it is rowdy, will eventually correct the behavior.

## Patience

A key factor in persuading your pig to behave in a certain manor is *patience*. Pigs do not tolerate abusive, rough treatment well. If you are impatient and irritated before a training session is about to begin, you will get nowhere with the pig. Prepare for each lesson by providing a time and place where there will be no outside interference for you or the pig. Eliminate anything that could distract you or the pig, such as visitors, spectators, other pigs or animals, television, radio, and telephone.

Take a few minutes for the pig to change gears from what it was doing and for you to clear your mind. Prepare a tentative and flexible schedule for your lesson ahead of time. The actual flow of exercises will be determined by the strength and correctness of the pig's reactions to the stimuli you will be giving it. If at any time you become angry, frustrated, or disappointed in your pig's performance, it is better to stop for a few hours or for the day. End every training session on a positive note; persuade the pig to do something you know it does well, so the session can end with a reward.

## Discipline

Never scold your pig when you want to get a positive reaction. Force or discipline does not work well with pigs unless you want to *stop* a certain behavior. For example, if you want a pig to climb a set of stairs, you cannot force it to do so by dragging it up the stairs or hitting it on the rump. The pig will put on the brakes or back up instead of going forward. The pig's body is not as flexible as a dog's body, so climbing is more difficult. This is a pig fact of life! But a few grapes placed strategically on the stairs will give it a reason to expend the extra effort. On the other hand, a house pig that tries to put its sharp hooves on the sofa can be disciplined with a light tap on the snout and a firm "No." After a few attempts, the pig will understand that hooves on the sofa means something negative will happen to its tender nose.

## Initial Training

### Picking Up the Pig

Unless handled daily from birth, most pigs hate to be picked up, and they hate even more

A pig must feel secure when its legs are off the ground. Handle the pig every day, cradling it in your arms and using only as much pressure as is needed to keep the pig safe. Gently scratch its sides and talk to it in a kind voice.

to be restrained. You will believe this when you pick up your pig and find out that it can scream so loud and so long you wished you were wearing earplugs. If your pig has not been handled a lot, you must exercise great patience and gentleness. If you have followed the guidelines in "Bringing Your New Pig Home," pages 17–22, your pig is now coming to you for treats. Encourage it climb into your lap as you sit on the floor. Using the pig's favorite blanket on your lap will encourage it further. When the pig is comfortably sitting in your lap, gradually scratch and rub its whole body, and modify this by lightly cupping your arms around its bottom and front. Add pressure gradually over a period of lessons. When the pig is comfortable with a reasonable amount of pressure, cup your arms firmly around its rear and front, and scoop it up a few inches. Then immediately put it down. Repeat this a few times over several lessons. Eventually, take the plunge and stand up, with the pig in your arms. If the pig is comfrtable with this, repeat the lesson often, giving food and petting rewards for quiet behavior. If, no matter what you do, the pig screams, go back to square one and start the gentlying lesson again. When you can hold the pig in your arms, stroke its head and talk to it gently. Remind it that it is safe in your arms and you are not a lion ready to devour it.

## A Note About Screaming

A pig that does not want to be restrained will usually scream until it is put down. The scream of a jet engine at takeoff has been measured at 113 decibels, while the scream of a frightened pig has been measured at 115 decibels.

There are two things to consider when your pig is screaming:

1. Porcine Stress Syndrome (see full expla-

nation under First Aid.) A pig that is screaming can become very stressed.

2. Reinforcing the screaming behavior by putting the pig down. The pig has been rewarded, and the screaming will continue every time you pick it up until you put it down.

For these reasons, it is imperative that you take the time to teach your pig that being held is not as bad as it seems.

## Overhandling

A pig that is handled too much or is never left alone can become a problem pig when it gets older, because it may be very demanding and unpleasant. Do not constantly give your pig treats, or you will become a "food machine" to it. When the food stops, it will begin nudging and then become rougher when the food does not appear. Be sure your pig has time alone during which it can play with toys, investigate the room or yard, and become mentally active.

## Housebreaking

When you take your pig outside for the first time and every time thereafter, plan to stay with it until it is finished with its toilet duties. If you have a wonder pig that performs the first time, you should be ready to praise it. Be sure that the pig is *not* praised until it is finished. While it is "going," tell it to "go potty" or whatever other terms you wish to use. No matter what words you pick, use those exclusively from then on. When it is finished, say, "Good pig!" Be sure you stay outside with the pig until it has relieved itself; this means both urination and bowel movement. Give the pig the verbal command for both. If the pig does

not do both, put it in a small controlled area until it does. Bringing the pig inside before it is finished can result in "reverse housebreaking"—the pig will relieve itself almost immediately upon entering the house. Giving treats as a reward may cause the pig to stop before it is finished in order to receive the treat. Then, when the pig enters the house, it may relieve itself again.

To persuade your pig to use the litter box in the house, try taking a small piece of fecal matter from outside and placing it in the litter box. Normally, this will keep the pig from using the litter box as a bed. For pigs that are very fastidious, you may need a litter box for the outside pen as well. Be prepared to watch your pig's attitude. Be sure the litter box is large enough to permit the pig to enter and turn around comfortably. Otherwise, the pig may have its front feet in the box and the business end outside. If the pig does not use the litter box where you placed it, try another place or an additional litter box. If the pig makes a mistake, do not pick it up or it will forget what it was in the middle of doing.

Usually, the pig is ready to be introduced to other portions of the house within a month. Still, you may find that your pig has occasional accidents when it has full run of the house. Placing one or two more litter boxes throughout the house will help alleviate the problem.

Giving your pig access to the outside pen via a doggie door can be the answer to your problems. However, think about what you will do in rainy weather. If your pig's outside pen has a dirt surface, you may not be too happy if it rains and your pig finds mud bathing is good fun. If your pig's outside pen is concrete, be sure its bed is free of drafts and can be kept dry in wet weather, or it may lead to the development of arthritic diseases.

Spayed females and barrows are the easiest to house-train. Boars will mark the house indiscriminately all the time. Sows will "forget" they are housebroken when they cycle, which is usually every 21 days. They, too, will leave small "marks" here and there, just in case a boar happens to drop in for a visit and is looking for romance.

If your pig has a relapse and suddenly seems "unhousebroken," do not try to overcompensate. Instead, find out if something is different in its normal routine or environment. Watch for behavior changes. Some pigs do not like changes in their routine.

## Stain and Odor Removal

When your pet pig does have an accident, this section will help you in removing the evidence.

A pig's bowel movement is rarely a problem, because it is normally firm and easy to pick up. But if the pig has a loose movement, carpets and fabrics can be stained. Follow these three steps to remove stains caused by urine or a loose bowel movement from carpet or clothing:

- Sponge and soak up as much of the liquid as possible. Do not rub the fabric, or you may press the stain more deeply into the fibers.
- Apply a generous amount of plain club soda to the area and let it stand about five minutes.
- Soak up as much of the club soda as possible.
- Cover the area generously with cornstarch.
- Let it stand twenty-four hours. You should see the stain rise into the cornstarch.
- Vacuum.

If the stain persists, repeat the applications of club soda and cornstarch. Full-strength (3 percent) hydrogen peroxide may also be used.

Try some on a hidden portion of the carpet first to see if there is any bleaching action to the fabric itself.

## Establishing House Rules

House rules are established and reinforced by two methods: distraction and discipline.

When your pig exhibits a behavior you do not want, first try the gentler approach—distracting the pig. If the pig is chewing on a book, offer it a toy, scratch its side, or make a loud noise. This solution usually proves to be temporary, and the pig will at a future date resume the unwanted behavior. However, if you give it a light tap on the nose combined with a verbal "No," the behavior will stop immediately. If the behavior resumes, it should be followed by another tap and a "No." Very soon, the pig will associate the "No" with a tap on the nose, and unwanted behaviors can usually be corrected with a single word. In the wild, if a piglet aggravates the mother, she disciplines with a loud grunt and a nip. The mother pig is usually very definite to her

Your piglet should be exposed to children and young non-aggressive animals such as puppies and kittens. This will teach it to have a friendly attitude towards them as it matures.

# Training Your Pig

young that she is not happy with their behavior, and she usually gets the message across in one or two sessions. If you teach your pig at an early age that it must respect the word "No," you will save yourself a lot of grief and energy. It is extremely important that the tap you administer to the pig is not hurtful to the pig, but merely to command its attention. You should *never* slap, hit, or otherwise be physically abusive. Not only is this inhumane treatment, but a pig will totally forget what it is you are displeased about. It will develop a total case of amnesia about the matter, remembering only that you hurt it. Pigs have excellent memories, so remember that when you administer discipline.

A pig must learn at an early age that biting or snapping is not acceptable behavior. This is another instance of the need for discipline. Although pigs have individual personalities and most never bite, occasionally a pig will bite out of fear or anger. This behavior must be stopped immediately. If caught at an early age, most pigs will never repeat nipping again. If the bad habit is not stopped, it could become an established behavior that is nearly impossible to break. When and if your pig bites or nips you for any reason, correct the behavior immediately and firmly with a light smack on the nose. At the same time, tell it "No" in a very loud and displeased voice. The pig must know that you will never tolerate this behavior.

Another pig behavior that is not desirable and must be stopped is rooting on items that are not theirs, such as clothing, furniture, books, plants, and walls. A bored pig is more likely to get into trouble in these areas. First, try to give your pig some attention. If you take it for a walk daily, have a small training session, or put it through maneuvers it knows well, there will be less undesirable behavior. To distract it, give it some toys of its own and

some blankets and towels to push around. Take the time to play with your pig. You can teach it to retrieve a ball, a knotted sock, or a toy. The pig will get some exercise for its mind and its body, and you do not have to worry about tiring it out. A pig will quit when it has had enough.

Discipline can be a tap on the nose accompanied by a "No." If you are some distance away when the pig misbehaves, you must use another method until the pig understands and will respond to the "No." Outdoors, a child's water pistol can be used to discourage rooting, chewing, or other unwanted behavior. If your pig happens to be a water-loving soul, add lemon juice to the water at the rate of three tablespoons to a pint of water. Try to squirt the pig in the mouth, avoiding the eyes if possible. The tart flavor will distract the pig from what it is doing and give you time to redirect its energies. Be sure to say "No" a second before the water hits its mouth; timing is critical.

If you are indoors and want to correct an unwanted behavior, try the following method. Put six or eight marbles in a used aluminum soft-drink can and tape the opening shut with duct tape. When the pig needs discipline and you are not close to it, toss the can in its direction, immediately preceding its impact with the word "No." Again, timing is critical. Whether you use the water pistol or the can, the pig will soon learn to associate the word "No" with correction and will cease the unwanted act when it hears the word. The key here is persistence and *consistency* on your part. You may have to carry the water pistol in your pocket or have several cans lying around the rooms to which the pig has access. In any event, be sure you have some method of backing up your displeasure and getting the message across to the pig every time. Eventually, you will have to use the pistol or can

# *Training Your Pig*

only occasionally to reinforce your position; "No" will be sufficient.

## Teaching Tricks and Amazing Feats

Do training sessions every day, and follow with the pig's regular meal. It is difficult to keep from overrewarding when the pig does something very amazing, but a small bit of fruit or other food will get a better result than a large one.

## Come

This is the first thing you should teach your pig, since it will be a prerequisite for other training. Stand about five feet in front of your pig and show it the treat in your hand. Call its name, and say "Come." When it arrives in front of you, immediately give it the treat, say "Good pig," and pat its head. Back up another five feet and repeat the original command and sequence. Repeat this about five times. The next day, increase the distance slightly. If the pig does not immediately respond, try getting its attention by putting some of its regular food in a small plastic bowl with a lid that will make noise when you shake it.

## Harness Training

Harness training is another prerequisite to the teaching of tricks. It can begin before the pig is gentled, although it is a little easier on the pig if you have accustomed it to its new area. If your pig is not fully grown, an adjustable harness is the wisest investment. Until the pig is fully grown, you will probably need several changes of harness. It is very important that the harness fits very snugly, or the pig will be able to back out of it. There are two types

To insure the proper fit of your pig's harness, you will need two measurements. Place the tape on top of the withers and measure all the way around in *front* of the front legs. From the same point, measure all the way around *behind* the front legs. Buy an adjustable harness with these measurements as a guide.

of harnesses, the figure eight and the "H" style. The figure eight is the correct type to order for a miniature pig. You will need two measurements to get an exact fit for your pig. Place the tape measure on top of the withers (see conformation drawing, page 84, for their location), bring it around and in front of the front legs, and back up to the withers. For the second measurement, start at the same place, but bring the tape under and around, behind the front legs and back to the starting place. When you order a harness, give these two measurements, and tell the supplier you want both pieces adjustable, with your measurements as the tightest fit. Ordered this way, your harness will last longer. Also, be sure the supplier has the easy release snaps instead of buckles.

**Putting on the Harness:** Measure your pig, and adjust the harness ahead of time. If the pig is gentle, let it climb into your lap. Slowly and gently, put the harness over its head, reassuring it that this is not an awful trick. Put the harness in place, closing the front snap, which is less restrictive, first, and then the back one. Continue to reassure the pig, distracting it with a treat or two.

If the pig is not gentled yet, put the harness

# *Training Your Pig*

Offer your pig a treat through the neck opening of the harness. Do not try to put harness completely on in one lesson. Go slowly. After your pig accepts the harness over its neck, drop a few treats to keep it busy while you fasten the harness behind its back legs. Be sure the harness is adjusted to the correct measurement *before* you begin.

over your wrist, with a treat in your hand. When the pig takes the treat, slip the harness over its neck. Scatter a small amount of feed on the ground, and continue attaching the harness.

If the pig is calm, at this point, consider yourself fortunate. A more common reaction is like something from a full-blown pig rodeo. The pig will buck and pitch and carry on. Extreme caution must be exercised to ensure that the pig does not get stressed, overheated, and go into shock. There have been cases of pigs becoming very ill, and at least one case of a pig dying, following a violent reaction to being harnessed. It the pig's reaction is exceptionally strenuous, immediately remove the harness and watch for any physical problems.

Keep the pig in a confined area until it is no longer objecting to the harness. Check to see that there are no hooks or loose wires in the area that could catch the ring on the top of the harness. If the pig is calm, attach a short leash to the ring on top of the harness and let the pig drag it around. Be absolutely certain that the leash cannot catch on anything.

Gentle, unhurried leash training is the easiest on both you and your pig. Offering treats may be hard on your back in the beginning, but will help to give your pig a positive attitude towards being restrained by a leash.

When the pig is calm and has accepted both the harness and leash, you can use one of two methods, or a combination of them, to train your pig to walk on a leash. Do not assume that because the pig is no longer objecting to the restraints you can start walking it like a dog. The minute you put pressure on the harness, the pig will probably balk and begin to fight.

**Walking on a Leash, Method One:** This is an easy method for preliminary harness training, because it gives you two hands free. Pick a section of your yard that lacks trees, bushes, or objects of any kind for a twenty-foot diameter. Check to see that some shade covers at least part of the circle. Pound a three-foot section of metal pipe about halfway into the ground in its center. The pipe should be strong, smooth, and free of burrs. Take a ten-foot nylon leash that has a hand loop on one end and a strong clip on the other. Slip the looped end of the leash over the pipe. Stretch the leash to its full extension and walk to the outermost limits of the leash. Be sure it cannot get caught on anything and the loop moves freely around the pipe. Put a water dish within reach, but not where the pig can get tangled.

# *Training Your Pig*

Attach the clip to the ring on the top of the harness.

Stay with the pig for several sessions to be sure that it does not have a violent reaction. The pig should already be used to the harness and the leash, but not to the restraint they cause. Scatter some feed in a trail from the center to the outermost limits of the leash. Most pigs will be distracted with searching for the food and will not mind being tethered. Occasionally, a very wild pig will run and hit the end of the leash and find there is nowhere else to go when it comes to a jarring stop. Since you are near, removal of the leash might be necessary if the pig is very upset. Do not leave during this critical period, or the pig could become injured or stressed. Leave the pig on the leash for about thirty minutes the first time, and increase to an hour the next day. If you use this method for preliminary training, you may find this type of restraint helpful when you are on outings and need to restrict your pig's freedom.

When the pig has become accustomed to the area, and to the limits of its temporary world, enter its circle with some treats. Walk next to the pig, bending over and offering the treats. When the pig becomes anxious for more treats, walk to the outside of the ring, offering the treats and forcing the pig to exert some pressure on the harness. Reinforce behavior that puts light pressure on the harness. Eventually, reinforce only when the pig walks next to you with little or no pressure on the harness. Practice this every day for several days. The pig is ready to walk next to you, with you holding the leash. See "Finishing on a Leash," below.

*A word of caution about restraint and confinement:* Do not consider restraining your pig an alternative to monitoring your pig. A pig restrained in any area is still dependent on you and totally at your mercy for its well-being.

Adequate shade and water should be available always. This can be a problem at times, and it might be hard to resist attaching the leash to a shade source such as a tree or bush. But, the pig may soon become entangled and stressed, and will not be able to escape predators such as loose dogs.

**Walking on a Leash, Method Two:** This method normally works only with very gentle pigs. It is a lot harder for you physically, and harder for the pig mentally, because the pig *knows* it is you on the other end of the leash.

Once it has become accustomed to wearing its harness and being attached to the lead, pick up the looped end, putting no pressure on harness, and talk to the pig. It will know you are at the other end, believe me. Do not be heavy-handed and pull, or it will balk, buck, and scream. This method takes much more patience, because you are constantly interacting with the pig. Offer treats and walk a step or two ahead. If necessary, throw a raisin or grape to the place you wish the pig to reach. This method will normally take several sessions, unless the pig is very docile. Try to do several sessions a day. Never let the pig develop the attitude that you are forcing it to come, or you will end up with a pig that will balk for a long time at the slightest pressure. Once the pig is coming to you and walking alongside of you, put very light pressure on the leash and offer treats. Now you are ready for finishing on a leash.

**Finishing on a Leash:** Switch to a leash four feet long. Reinforce all positive behavior when the pig walks next to you without putting excessive pressure on the harness. Keep the pig's attention with the treats, enticing it. You will know that your pig is motivated if its head is up searching for the food. Make right and left turns, circles with the pig on the inside, and circles with the pig on the outside. Try some

# *Training Your Pig*

about-face turns. When the pig is doing all this without fighting you, you are ready to take it away from home on a leash. Gradually expose the pig to new situations and environments. Most people that you meet will be happy to meet your new good citizen.

## Sit

Dazzle your friends by teaching your pig to sit, one of the easiest tricks for a pig to learn.

Pick a time of day when you are almost ready to feed your pig its next meal. Have a pocketful of treats ready. With both of you standing, facing each other, feed the pig one treat from your hand.

That one was for free. Now the "work" begins for the pig. The pig is now in a receptive mood, and knows you have treats. It will be easier to keep its attention. The pig should have its rear end against a wall (preferably a corner) or other solid object. Because a pig

When teaching the Sit, show the treat to the pig, and then partially conceal it within your fingertips to prevent nipping. Say "Sit" and guide the pig into a sit with this method. Give the treat immediately when the bottom touches the ground, and say, "Good Pig!"

has poor eyesight, show it the treat first, then hold it one foot above its head for a few seconds, say "Sit," and simultaneously, bring the treat about two inches over its nose and just slightly toward its eyes. Repeat the word "Sit" several times during the training process. As the pig reaches up for the treat, move the treat slightly toward its eyes but still just out of reach. When the pig goes into a sitting position (which will raise its nose an inch or two), give it the treat immediately, adding verbal praise. If the pig does not sit, *do not give it the reward*. It was not earned.

After the first actual "Sit," give the command "Sit" first, show the treat, and repeat the sequence above. Do not forget to reinforce the verbal command during the process until the pig actually sits. Then immediately administer the treat and follow with verbal praise.

Practice this until you see the pig is losing interest in the food or exercise, or about fifteen times, whichever comes first. Never burn a pig out on a particular exercise.

Gradually reduce the number of commands you give the pig, and start to insist that the pig sit upon verbal command. This may take only one day for some pigs, a week or more for others.

## Dance

Before teaching your pig to dance, it is very helpful if the pig has learned to sit. If you try to teach the dance trick first, the pig will have difficulty learning the sit trick. A very large pig, or any pig that is overweight for its size, will have much difficulty performing this trick. The rear legs will not have the strength and flexibility necessary to execute the dance. The best treats to use for this trick are strips of carrot, celery, or a similar vegetable.

Ask your pig to "Sit" following with a food

# *Training Your Pig*

To learn the dance the pig must be in good condition and not overweight. Having learned the Sit is very helpful. The pig must be offered a treat that is worth this monumental effort. The treat is offered just out of reach until the pig reaches the desired height. Do not expect full extension of the rear legs on heavily muscled pigs. When the pig is standing on its rear legs steadily, move the food just out of reach so the pig will take a step or two towards you.

reward. From the sitting position, show the pig the treat, holding it directly above and just out of reach of the pig's nose. Give the command "Dance" and keep the treat just out of reach. As the pig stretches for the treat, give the treat if the pig's front feet clear the floor by even half an inch. A pig in the wild can easily stand on its hind legs to harvest fruit from bushes and low trees—the behavior is natural. Slowly, over a period of several training sessions, demand that the pig stand up a bit higher before it gets the treat. Eventually, you will demand extension to full height. This is only possible for pigs in excellent condition, with little abdominal fat.

After many training sessions during which the pig stands in full extension, you are ready to put the finishing touches on the dance. With the pig hungry and encouraged to reach full

extension, move the food an inch out of its reach. If the pig takes even a slight step, immediately bring the treat to the pig and praise verbally. Do not forget the command word "Dance" before you give the treat.

Eventually, you can expect to ask your pig to take two or three steps. Any more than that is very difficult for the pig to accomplish. A little background music will add the final dimension to the atmosphere for your dancing pig.

## Kneel

This is a more difficult trick to teach, especially to a very hungry pig. It is best taught after another training session, when the pig is less apt to be frantic for food. With the pig's rear end against a solid object such as a wall, preferably a corner, show the pig the treat, say "Kneel," put the treat to the pig's nose, under its chin, and down to the floor. As the pig reaches for the food, try to block the animal from backing out of the corner, and move the treat along the floor toward its tummy. The pig will not be able to back up, and should kneel for the treat. This trick may have to be repeated often before the pig gets the message. Remember not to let the pig get the treat unless it kneels (which will be very difficult), or it will be rewarded for not performing the trick properly. If this method does not work for your pig, sit on the floor with your legs straight out in front of you. Put your right hand containing a treat under your right leg, just barely showing through on the inside of your leg. Show the pig the treat. It should go down on its front legs to get the treat. Do not let it have the treat unless it kneels.

Pigs kneel frequently as part of their natural behavior, but the reason the pig has more difficulty learning this trick is the close proximity of food—food that is not out of reach.

# *Training Your Pig*

## Climbing Stairs

Most pigs will not climb up or down stairs when introduced to them without very strong motivation. In many instances, each stair is taller than the pig is.

Going down steps is more difficult for a pig than going up the stairs. To teach "down the stairs," place treats at strategic locations in a trail down the steps. Leave the pig alone at the top. The treats should be within smelling distance, but just out of reach so that it has to at least partially climb the step to get it. Occasionally, two treats per step are necessary. The pig's appetite will soon help it overcome its fear and it will teach itself how to maneuver on the treacherous grade.

Often a first-timer will tumble down the steps, because the pig's body is not as flexible as most other animals' bodies. When they tumble, they usually bump their nose a few times, which adds to their negative attitude about the steps. If left alone, with tempting treats in strategic locations, they will figure it out themselves. Once they master the "down," it is time to teach "up the stairs." Place the pig at the bottom, and a trail of treats going up the stairs. Again, leave the pig alone. Within hours, your pig will be leaping up the stairs when it hears the food dish.

## Jumping over an Object

Prepare your training area by placing a 4-foot section of 3/4-inch PVC pipe on the ground. To make the pipe more noticeable, spiral black electrical tape around the pipe. With your pig on one side of the pipe, facing the other side, offer it a raisin , and tell it "Jump." Give the raisin to it after it has crossed completely over the pipe. Always follow the treat with verbal praise, and always use the same phrase for praise. Repeat this in

Two bricks with holes in them and a length a 3/4 (2 cm) inch plastic pipe are all that is needed to start your pig on its jumping career. The initial jump should be very low. Gradually increase the height over a long period of time. Pigs are not natural jumpers, so take your time. The bricks can be turned on end and the pipe raised one hole at a time as your pig becomes an expert.

both directions, turning it by keeping a treat in front of its face.

After this has been repeated 25 times, raise the pipe one inch. There are bricks available with three holes in them. They make nice stands for the pipe that can be raised one hole at a time. Place an end of the pipe through the bottom hole in the brick.

Do the same thing as before, offering the treat as it faces the direction you want it to go. When it is completely over the pipe, give the treat. Repeat 25 times. Stop for that session.

Gradually raise the pipe, one inch at a time, until it is about 8 inches off the ground. As the pipe gets higher, the pig may knock it off occasionally. When it knocks the pipe down, do not give the treat. Instead, use the treat to guide the pig back to the starting place, replace the pipe, and repeat the lesson.

# *Training Your Pig*

## Jumping Through a Hoop

After your pig is jumping the 8-inch-high pipe, you can substitute other articles, such as a hoop, (also striped by tape) by placing it directly in front of the pipe on the ground, at the same height. Eventually, remove the 4-foot section of pipe, and you have a pig jumping through a hoop. You can then raise it to the level that is the maximum your pig can jump.

Once your pig has mastered jumping, repeat the lesson by asking it to jump it three times a day.

For the safety of your pig's front legs and joints, do not ask it to jump too high. Do not train on hard surfaces, such as concrete or floors, that might promote slipping.

## Jumping Through a Solid Hoop

This is a variation of the above jumping routine. Once your pig has mastered the regular jumping through a hoop, hang strips of tissue paper from the top of the hoop and begin the training again. Each time you vary a routine, you should get the pig to perform it perfectly before you proceed to the next level. Once your pig has mastered jumping through the hoop with the strips of tissue paper, glue a solid piece of tissue paper on the hoop and tear a hole in the middle. Once it has mastered this, gradually reduce the hole to a tear and then to a solid piece of paper. In no time, your pig will be flying through the solid hoop like a real circus animal. When performing for the public, use flashy colors with strips hanging along the sides and edges.

## The Shell Game

This classic con game is a natural for a pig. Use three flowerpots or plastic cups. Put a treat under one, and show the pig where it is. Of course, the pig's natural instinct is to root out and "unearth" the treasure. This trick should be performed on grass to start so your pig can get under the pot to flip it over. Soon you will be shuffling the pots, and your "wonder pig" will find the right one without hesitation.

## Nose Tricks

There are countless other tricks you can teach your pig to do with its nose, such as pushing a barrel, closing and opening a door, turning on push-type switches, and more. Placing the treat near the desired response and rewarding as soon as the impatient nudging behavior starts will reinforce that behavior. This will take much patience, and the important thing is to reward at the precise moment the nudging behavior begins. Then gradually wait until the behavior begins to stop. When the behavior is repeated, reward and praise.

To teach pushing the barrel, put a small barrel on its side in front of the pig. Put a raisin behind the barrel and another raisin in front of the barrel. Direct your pig's nose there with another treat, telling it "Push." As the

To teach nose tricks, such as pushing the barrel, place a small treat in such a position that the pig must nudge the object you want moved or pushed. Place another treat behind the barrel, so that when it is moved, another treat is exposed. You can encourage further pushing by dropping treats behind the barrel. When the barrel is moved, another treat is exposed.

pig reaches for the raisin, the barrel will roll over the other raisin, exposing it to the pig. Try to drop another raisin on the other side of the barrel, so as the pig reaches for the second raisin and the barrel rolls, it will expose another raisin. Keep dropping raisins until you run out. Do not forget to remind your pig to "Push" as the lesson goes on.

Other nose tricks can be taught with "discover"-type toys, designed for preschool children, that have buttons, pull rings, etc. Be inventive and discover your pig's hidden talents.

## Playing the Piano or Cash Register

This nose trick is so cute and simple it deserves a section of its own. Many children's push-button toys will work for this trick— piano, pop-up toys, cash register, etc.

First place a few favorite treats (peanuts, raisins, etc.) on the piano keyboard. Coax the pig over to the piano and pick up a treat from the keyboard, making sure it sees where you got the treat. When you are removing the treat from the keyboard, push on a key and say "Play the piano," "Make music," or whatever command you wish your pig to associate with this trick.

Give the pig the treat. Repeat the process several times. By this time, the pig will most likely have trotted over to the piano and helped itself to the treats. As it is eating the treats, its normal behavior is to root slightly, and the pressure of its nose on the keyboard will create "music." Always praise it for its accomplishments. With some pigs, you must keep the treat in your fingers instead of putting it on the keyboard.

Once the pig has mastered this feat, you may wish to glue a toy candelabra on a baby grand, and change the pig's name to Pig-erace!

Guide the pig toward the see-saw board with a treat. Be sure the board is wide enough so all four feet are on the board. Slowly move the pig forward and give the treat before it reaches the middle. Increase the distance that the pig must travel on the board to get the treat gradually. When the pig has reached the middle, be sure that the board tips gradually so the pig is not frightened.

## Seesaw and Narrow Bridge

Your pig can be taught to walk up a seesaw or over a narrow bridge by holding a treat in front of the pig and telling it "Go up." Sometimes, a trail of treats on the board will work better. For the seesaw, have an assistant on the other side to keep the board from moving down too rapidly as the pig approaches the middle and changes the balance. Gradually increase the speed with which the board falls. Each time the pig approaches the middle, slow it down, so that there is a gradual change in the balance, and it will soon learn to do this itself. To start out, use a 4-inch-diameter piece of PVC sewer pipe and a 1-inch-by-12-inch board about 8 feet long. This provides a gradual slope and the pig is not afraid even the first time. When the pig has mastered that slope, you can gradually increase the height of the fulcrum or length of the board. In the learning stages, this lesson should be done on grass or carpet. This trick will be very helpful when you begin to teach your pig to climb a ramp into your car.

## The Pirouette

The pirouette is a small circular motion made by the pig standing in one spot. This trick can be taught by holding a treat just in front of the pig's nose and guiding it with the treat in a small circle. Be sure you use exaggerated hand movements and ask the pig to "Pirouette." The pig can learn to do this in either direction or both. The pig should not be rewarded unless the pirouette is performed completely.

## The Figure Eight

With your two feet approximately 30 inches apart, and the pig in front of you, ask the pig to do the "figure eight." For this trick, have a treat in each hand. Guide the pig through the middle of your legs with the treat brought from behind with one hand. As the pig reaches the front middle, make a smooth transition with the other treat in the other hand as you guide it through the middle again. When the pig reaches the completion of the figure eight, give it the treat. When the pig is proficient with the figure eight, a variation of the trick, called "Threading the Needle," can be performed as you are walking.

## Barrel Racing

If you have ever watched a barrel racer perform on a swift horse, you know the excitement as the horse heads for the finish line. You can teach your pig to run the barrels by placing three barrels in the cloverleaf position. Guide the pig with treats around each barrel in the proper direction. As the pig rounds the last barrel, run backward with the treat in front of you, and the pig will race across the finish line. It is imperative that the pig round each barrel in the proper direction and is not given the treat until it has completed the whole exercise correctly.

## Additional Training and Advanced Pigs

If you are motivated to further train your pig, try some experimenting by trying to modify the natural behaviors of your pet. You can use food rewards, as you have learned in the sections above. By being creative and inventive, you will discover many hidden talents in your little friend. Occasionally, training seminars are held in conjunction with pig-club events and shows. Enrolling in these educational programs and subscribing to pig fanciers' magazines will help keep you in touch with other people who enjoy training pigs. Share information and tips on things you have learned with other enthusiasts to broaden your knowledge and expertise. Subscribe to a pig-training newsletter, in which ideas are shared.

# *Identifying and Showing Your Pig*

## Identification

Your pig should be identified by some permanent means. You will need this identification if you plan to show your pig. And if your pig is lost or stolen, you will have a means of proving your claim.

## Tattooing

Two types of tattooing equipment are available. The most common type is a pliertype apparatus. It has slots to fit a series of letters or numbers with needle points that puncture the ear when applied. Ink is then rubbed into the wounds made by the needle points. Since the ink that is used is dark, it is diffiuclt to read on dark pigs. This type of tattoo is temporarily very painful to the pig

The other tattoo method involves an electrically operated tattoo gun or pen. The tattoo is applied freehand, and can be done in white and various colors. The difficult part of this procedure is keeping a nonanesthetized pig still enough to apply a legible tattoo.

## Microchip Implants

This is the new, high-tech way of identifying pigs and other animals. A microchip is inserted into a special syringe and implanted through the skin into a muscle at a location designated by the owner. If the microchips are implanted into the muscle with a ver-heavy-gauge syringe, a local or general anesthetic may be necessary. Most often, these devices are implanted subcutaneously and thus do not require anesthesea. A special digital scanner is used to read the microchip identification number. Microchips implanted in young pigs often become "lost" in the fatty tissues and become deeply embedded. If you do have a microchip inserted in a young pig, have it checked periodically to see if it is still readable.

## Ear Tags

This is a highly visible way to identify pigs. Colors or numbers are used, but this method can prove unsightly and can be injurious due to biting by other pigs or rubbing of the affected ear. A hole will be left where the ear tag punctured the ear cartilage. Most people with pet pigs do not like the ear tag method. Also, if the pig is stolen, the thief merely has to cut off the ear tag and tattoo the pig with a different number.

## Freeze-Branding

This method is similar to the old-style cattle/horse branding, except that hot irons are not used. Instead, a copper brand is immersed in liquid nitrogen to $-270$ degrees and applied to the skin on a shaved area of the animal. It is as painless as picking up an ice cube that sticks to your fingers. The hair grows in white where the brand was applied. Of course, this method is not suitable on white or light-colored pigs.

## Naming Your Pet Pig

| Pig Theme | Celebrity Theme | Misc. Theme |
|---|---|---|
| Olympig | Cary Grunt | Boarin' To |
| Pace Pigcante | Basil Ham- | Love |
| Pigalily | bone | Pen Pal |
| Piganinni | Gloria Van- | Sow What |
| Pig-a-rachee | dergilt | Spam-a-la |
| Pig-a-sus | Merle Hog- | Rhoda Rooter |
| Pigfoot | gard | |
| Piggy Sue | Peggy Su-Wee | |
| Pig-Me | Sir Thomas | |
| Pig-nay-shus | Bacon | |
| Pignic | Smell Tillis | |
| Pig-o-my-heart | | |
| Pig-ski | | |
| Pigture Perfect | | |

# *Identifying and Showing Your Pig*

Picking a name for your pet pig can prove to be lots of fun for your friends and family. The whimsical aspect of owning a pet as unusual as a pig, combined with the animal's smile-provoking appearance, justifies some of the most humorous choices. At this time, there are countless pigs named Arnold, Priscilla, and Penelope. These names are comparable to Fuzzy, Fluffy, and Tiger for cats, and Rover, King, and Princess for dogs. But with a little ingenuity and research, you can come up with a name with real Pig-a-nality.

## Starting a Mini–Pig Club in Your Area

If there are several pig enthusiasts in your area, you might want to start a small pig club. For a club to operate efficiently and stay that way, it needs dedicated people willing to give of their time and expertise.

If you live in an area with a medium to large population of miniature pigs, you also might want to consider starting a club of your own. You can obtain a membership list of pig lovers in your area when you become a member of the North American Potbellied Pig Association (NAPPA) or the National Committee on Potbellied Pigs (NCOPP). A few letters and phone calls can be made to those living in the geographical area where you wish to establish a club. Most pig lovers want to share stories and learning experiences, and a club is a good place for comradeship, education, and fun. If you pick a motto reflecting your expectations, and live by it, your club should thrive. It can put on fun, educational, and show events.

## Showing Your Pet Pig

### What Is a Judge Looking for in a Pig?

The following information is an explanation of what a NAPPA judge is looking for when he or she is placing pigs at a NAPPA-sanctioned show;. If you know what the judge will have in mind, you will soon know how to pick out your best pigs to take to the show. Knowing what a judge is looking for will also help you pick proper sires and dams for your offspring. It will help help you pick out pigs to buy for show and breeding and help you decide which animals you produce should be sold as show-potential pigs, or as neutered pigs to those desiring a pet.

With these criteria in mind, it is fun to sit ringside and "place" animals yourself and compare your choices to those of the judge. This way you will learn to judge structure and movement. If your choices are different from the judge's, it is not good etiquette to question him or her about decisions. Often, with very close competitions, judgment calls are made that would be hard for the novice to understand or agree with. *It is one person's opinion, that day!* Respect the judge's authority and do not question his or her decisions.

## The NAPPA Standard Pig-Judging Guide.

The following information, courtesy of NAPPA (North American Potbellied Pig Association) , illustrates the distribution of points for structure and movement.

# *Identifying and Showing Your Pig*

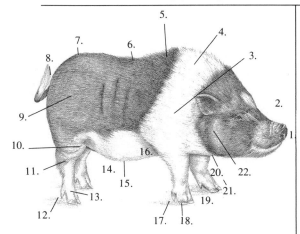

The front legs should be straight and wide-set with the toes pointing straight forward.

The pig should be well-balanced with moderate sway of back and pot belly.

1. Snout 2. Face 3. Neck 4. Shoulder 5. Heart Girth 6. Back 7. Rump 8. Tail Set 9. Ham 10. Stifle 11. Hock 12. Dewclaw, rear 13. Pastern, rear 14. Rear Flank 15. Underline 16. Fore Flank 17. Dewclaw, front 18. Hoof 19. Pastern, front 20. Knee 21. Jowl 22. Cheek

## Head—5 Points

**Eyes:** Deep, not bugged, wide-set, clear.

**Bite:** The bite of a pig is not like that of a dog or a horse. The teeth are not required to meet precisely. The important consideration of the bite is that it is not undershot or overshot. Extremely short noses are sometimes by an undershot bite.

**Nose:** Short to medium length. The nose structure shall be within an acceptable range of length and arch. A nose that turns somewhat to the side is considered a fault. Nostrils must allow for free passage of air while at rest. Wheezing, snoring, excessive sneezing, or nasal discharge is considered a fault.

## Front End Assembly—10 Points

**Neck:** Reasonably short, solid, carrying head properly.

**Chest:** Wide, deep, proper spring of ribs.

**Shoulders:** Well developed, symmetrical.

## Leg Structures—15 Points

**Legs:** Sturdy, reasonably heavily boned.

**Front Stance:** Wide-set, straight through the knee, standing well on pasterns.

**Rear Leg Set:** Wide-set, standing well on hocks and pasterns. Viewed from the rear, the hocks should be straight or slightly pointed inward, but not close or touching.

**Feet:** Two toes of even length pointing straight forward, with two properly developed dewclaws.

## Back Body—10 Points

**Vulva:** Proper size and placement.

**Testicles:** Both present, proper size and development for age.

**Teats:** At least five in each line, evenly spaced, the total number may be odd. On boars and barrows, the last one or two teats in each line may be closer together and close to the center.

**Rump:** On females and barrows, the rump should be rounded and gently sloped. Boars may have a less rounded and somewhat steeper rump.

# *Identifying and Showing Your Pig*

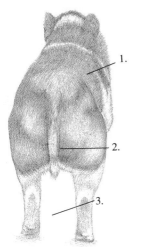

The hocks should point straight backwards or slightly inwards, and be moderately far apart.

1. Turn over the top   2. Depth of crotch   3. Width

## POTBELLY CHARACTERISTICS

**Face, Jowls, Nose, Ears—10 Points**
**Face:** Wide, full in proportion.
**Nose:** Short to medium in length, various degrees of arch are acceptable.
**Jowls:** Obvious, and in proportion to head.
**Ears:** Small, erect, somewhat flat.

## Back, Belly, Tail—10 Points

**Back:** The sway of the back should be moderate and in proportion to the length. Long-bodied pigs should have more sway than cobby ones. ("Cobby" means short back, heavy trunk, short legs.) Cobbyness is a desirable trait, so length must be considered in evaluating sway.
**Belly:** Viewed from the side, the belly should be obviously rounded but not exaggerated or touching the ground. Viewed from the top, the belly should not round from the backbone and should have only slight lateral protuberance.
**Tail:** Straight, of medium length, with a switch on the end, active.

## Stature—10 Points

**Size:** Ideal has been established as 14 inches or less at the high point of the shoulders at one year of age.
**Presence:** Posture and poise of an animal in the ring adds a "presence" which is considered part of stature.

## General Appearance—15 Points

This includes motion and disposition. In this section the judge will consider how all the parts of the animal come together. Defects that are penalized in their own section may be further penalized in this section to whatever extent the judge sees fit. One severe fault may result in the deduction of all points in this section.

## Disposition—5 Points

Tractable. Friendly. Calm and not high strung.

## Movement—10 Points

Smooth-flowing motion providing ease of travel, free of irregular movements. Senior pigs are not expected to have as much spring as Junior pigs.

## Color—Zero Points

As long as the animal conforms to the NAPPA Standard, color and/ or markings shall in no way be a determining factor in placement in conformation classes.
**NOTE: CONDITION, QUALITY, AND TYPE ARE THE MOST IMPORTANT POINTS IN JUDGING.**

# Identifying and Showing Your Pig

## Tips for Showing Your Pet Pig

Now that you know what the judge is looking for, you will be taking your best pig(s) into the show ring in hopes of taking home the blue or even the purple ribbon. The following pointers will help you present your pig and yourself to your best advantage!

- Dress conservatively. Do not wear jeans, shorts, sandals, or any clothing that will cause attention to be focused on you instead of your pigs. Girls, that means no ultrashort or -tight skirts, etc. Wear pleasant but not loud colors. (For miniature-pig shows that are part of large livestock shows, check to see if NAPPA has granted special dispensation for dress code to comply with general overall dress code of the livestock show.) Remember, the judge is judging your pig!
- Practice good grooming for yourself as well as your pig. Be sure both of you are neat and "crisp" in appearance.
- Use a black leash and halter.
- Be sure your pig is well trained to the leash and halter and will focus on the treats when you need it "stacked" and showing off its pretty little body and face. Be sure it does not jump or stand on its hind legs for the treats.
- Read the judges' guidelines and show rules thoroughly, so you are informed as you step into the ring.
- Enter the ring with a smile, and keep a pleasant attitude.
- Be confident you have the best pig.
- Keep one eye on the judge, the other on your pig. *Always* keep your pig between you and the judge. Never block the judge's view of your animal.
- When the judge is looking at your pig, keep an eye on the pig, stay serious but pleasant, and watch for a signal from the judge to move your pig.
- Be courteous to other exhibitors as well as the judge and ring attendants. Remember, good sportsmanship begins with you.
- Keep your pig away from other pigs. Remember, the other pigs will probably be strangers to your pig and both may be curious, or may be aggressive. Always be aware of what your pig is doing!
- When the judge asks you to move, keep moving until he tells or motions you to stop. Stop where he indicates, keeping your pig a good distance away from the judge and other pigs and exhibitors.
- Bring treats for your pig, and keep them tucked away in a pocket.
- Study the anatomy of your pig and learn the names of each part. Many judges ask you to indicate a part of a pig to see how much you really know.
- If it is a warm day, keep a small spritzer bottle of water handy to spray your little friend down.
- Be ready when the judge motions to move pigs into placement position.
- Be gracious no matter what place your pig wins. Never grumble to anyone in or around the ring about your placement or the placement of other pigs. Never question the judge in the ring. If there is a social gathering afterward, you might ask the judge for his opinion about your pig, but don't expect him to remember every pig that day.
- Remember, the *judge's opinion is the only one that counts that day*, so give yourself and others a break, and don't bellyache after the show, about how it was poor judging, your pig was hot, you tripped, the judge only put up pigs belonging to pretty girls, and on and on. Remember, this is supposed to be fun. Let's keep the pig shows that way.

# Index

Abscesses, 37
Acclimation process, 21–22
Amino acids, 29–30
AMPA Standard, 14
Anatomy and physiology:
  dentition, 59–60
  digestive system, 62
  ears and hearing, 60
  eyes and vision, 60
  legs and feet, 61
  locomotion, 62
  muscles, 61
  nervous system, 60
  respiratory system, 62
  skeletal system, 61
  skin, 60–61
  snout and smell, 60
  urinary system, 62
Antibiotics, 31, 44

Barrow, 11
Bathing, 33–34
Behavior, 63–67
Bleeding, 51
Blue-green algae, 26
Boarding, 23
Boars, 8, 11
Body contact, 65
Bran, 31
Breeding:
  inbreeding, 13
  linebreeding, 13
Broken bones, 57
Buying. *See* Purchasing

Car travel, 25
Cleanliness, 64–65
Communication, 66
Conformation, 7–8
Crossbreed, 12
Cuts, 37

Dentition, 59–60
Dewclaws, 61
Diet. *See* Nutrition
Disease prevention:
  abscesses and cuts, 37
  antibiotic therapy, 44
  closed or semi-closed
    compounds and, 36

environmental conditions and,
  36–37
  medications, giving, 44, 47
  metabolic rates, normal, 37
  parasite control, 47–49
  signs of illness, 37
  temperature, taking, 37–38
  vaccination program, 42–44
  veterinarian trip, 38–39
  zoonoses, 49
  *See also* Diseases
Diseases:
  arthritic, 41
  baby big anemia, 42
  cholera, 42
  edema D, 42
  enteric salmonellosis, 42
  gastrointestinal, 39–40
  porcine proliferative enteritis,
    42
  reproductive, 41–42
  respiratory, 40–41
Dominance, social, 65
Dwarf, 14

Ear cleaning, 34–35
Ear tags, 82
Electrical shock, 57
Emergencies. *See* First aid
  emergencies
Environmental conditions, 36–37

Fat, 30
Feeding; Food. *See* Nutrition
Feet, 35, 61
First aid emergencies, 50
  airway problems, 50–51
  bleeding, 51
  broken bones, fractures,
    dislocations, 57
  convalescent treatment, 58
  electrical shock, 57
  heatstroke, 57
  poisoning, 51–54, 57
  prevention of, 58
  shock, 51
  stress and, 58
  wounds, 57–58
Freeze-branding, 82
Fruits, 31

Gilts, 8, 11
Grooming:
  bathing, 33–34
  ear cleaning, 34–35
  hoof care, 35
  teeth, 33

Harness training, 73–74
Health, 7
Health guarantee, 7
Hearing, 60
Heatstroke, 57
Hooves, 35, 61
Housebreaking, 70–71
Housing:
  acclimating pig to, 21–22
  indoor environment, 17–18
    food and water dishes, 18–19
    house-training readiness, 18
    nursery setup, 19–20
    pig-proofing house, 18
  outdoor environment, 20
    outside pen setup, 21
    pig-proofing yard, 20
    water access, 20–21
    weather, protection from, 20

Identification, 82
Iron supplement, 32

Language, 65
Leash, walking on, 74–76
Life expectancy, 5–6
Locomotion, 62

Medications:
  injections, 47
  liquids, 44, 47
  powders, 47
  tablets, 44
Metabolic rates, 37
Microchip implants, 82
Midget, 14
Mind of pig, 66–67
Minerals, 30
Miniature pigs:
  breeds of, 14
    African pygmy (Guinea hog),
      15
    Juliani (painted miniature), 15

# Index

Ossabaw Island (feral), 16
Vietnamese (potbellied), 15
Yucatan (Mexican hairless), 16
dwarf, 14
midget, 14
standards (AMPA), 14
taxonomy of, 16

Naming a pig, 82–83
NAPPA Standard, 83–85
Neutering, 11
Nursery, setting up, 19–20
Nutrition, 29
  amounts to feed, 31–32
  diet, basic, 30–31
  food components, 29–30
  how to feed, 32
  water, need for, 26, 29

Odor removal, 71
Overhandling, 70

Parasites:
  external, 49
  internal, 48–49
Pedigree, 12
Pelleted food, 29, 30, 31
Pets (other) and pigs, 17
Physiology. See Anatomy and
  physiology
Picking up, 69
Pig-sitter, 23
Plants, poisonous, 54, 57
Play, 64
Poisoning, 51–52
  from plants, 54, 57
  types of, 52–54
Protein, 29–30

Purchasing:
  evaluating pig as potential pet, 5–6
  health and conformation and, 6–8
  more than one pig, 11
  registered pig, 12-13
  sex and, 8, 11
  sources for, 6
  temperament and, 6
Purebreed, 12

Quarantine, 36

Registration, 12–13
Rooting, 63

Scent marking, 8, 11
Scratching, 63–64
Screaming, 69–70
Selenium, 32, 54
Sex, 8, 11
Shock, 51
Showing, 83–86
Sideswiping, 66
Skin, 60–61
Smell, sense of, 60
Sows, 8, 11
Spaying, 11
Stain removal, 71
Standards (AMPA), 14
Stress, 58

Tattooing, 82
Taxonomic classification, 16
Teeth:
  care of, 33
  eruption of, 59
  needle, 33
  tusks, 33, 59
Temperament, 6

Temperature, 37–38
Toilet areas, defined, 64
Training:
  advanced, 81
  barrel racing, 81
  climbing stairs, 78
  "come," 73
  "dance," 76–77
  disciplining, 68–69
  figure eight, 81
  harness and leash, 73–76
  housebreaking, 70–71
  house rules, 71–73
  jumping, 78–79
  "kneel," 77
  nose tricks, 79–80
  overhandling, 70
  patience for, 68
  picking up pig, 69
  pirouette, 81
  playing piano or cash register, 80
  ramps, walking up, 80–81
  reward, proper way to, 68
  screaming, 69–70
  "sit," 76
Travel, 24–25

Vaccination program, 42–44
Vegetables, 31
Veterinarian, 38–39
Vision, 60
Vitamins, 30

Wallowing, 21, 63
Water, 26, 29
Wild (feral) pigs, 16
Wounds, 57–58

Zoonoses, 49

## Addresses and Literature

North American Potbellied Pig Association
P.O. Box 784
Columbia, Missouri 65205

This organization is the coordinator between the two main potbelly pig registries (which follow) and are the developers of the standard of perfection and judging guidelines.

Potbelly Pig Registry Service, Inc., and American Miniature Pig Registry
22819 Stanton Road
Lakeville, Indiana 45636

International Potbelly Pig Registry
P.O. Box 277
Pescadero, California 94060

The above two registries have wonderful newsletters and other publications.

National Committee on Potbellied Pigs
10717 Citrus Drive
Moorpark, California 93021

This organization is a registry and also sanctions its own shows.

Pet Pig Training Quarterly
P.O. Box 1837
Grass Valley, California 95945

This newsletter is highly recommended for owners of pet pigs.